A SURVIVOR'S FIGHT FOR HEALING, JUSTICE, AND DNA REFORM

JULIE WEIL

First Hardback and Paperback Edition

Published by Freiling Agency, LLC.

P.O. Box 1264
Warrenton, VA 20188

www.FreilingAgency.com

HB ISBN: 978-1-969826-38-2
PB ISBN: 978-1-969826-37-5
E-book ISBN: 978-1-969826-39-9

Contents

1

Meeting Miami

IT WAS A CRISP FALL evening in 1978, and my mom, dad, little brother Jimmy, and I lived in the suburbs of Chicago. My father had just returned home from an uncharacteristic work trip that had kept him out of town for several weeks. As he walked into the house, I ran and jumped into his arms. Then he broke the news. "Jules, this is so exciting! I found a house for our family to live in, and it's in sunny Florida." He explained that the bank he worked for was opening its first office in that state, and that we were moving to a city called Miami. I could feel his unbridled enthusiasm as I innocently asked him to describe what "his- Ami" was like. I had never heard of this place before, and my seven-year-old self had not intentionally made the play on words. My dad laughed robustly and began describing a warm place with beaches, palm trees, and—most importantly—no snow.

Winter break quickly arrived, and it was set that we would be moving to Miami after spending one more Christmas in my parents' hometown of Davenport, Iowa. I was sad to be leaving my best friend, Michelle, who lived a few doors down from me in Chicago, and all of the extended family we had a couple of hours away in Iowa. All four of my grandparents had gone to the same high school together, and, subsequently, so had most of my aunts and uncles.

We were, and still are, a close-knit Midwestern family that really enjoys being together.

To ease my anxiety about moving away from friends and family, my dad kept showing me pictures of our new house in Miami. I loved seeing photos of where we would be living, mainly because it happened to be right across the street from what would be my new elementary school and a brand-new park. Moving meant I no longer had to walk to school bundled up in heavy jackets or snow pants. We were going to have a swimming pool in our backyard and could go to the beach whenever we wanted, even in wintertime.

Following the Christmas holidays, my family left for South Florida. A historic Midwestern blizzard rolled into Illinois and Iowa just as we were leaving, almost like a going-away party hosted by Mother Nature. In hindsight, I think it was a divine affirmation for my dad that he was making the right move. The initial trip into our new neighborhood remains indelibly etched in my memory, a vivid childhood tableau of new sights. Entering the house for the first time, I recall the sunny yellow front-hallway wallpaper, the coolness of the air conditioning on my pale skin, and the breathtaking view of the pool through the living room's sliding glass doors. I felt like I was in the movies, not knowing that this was just everyday living in our new neighborhood, about 45 minutes south of downtown Miami.

My bedroom, nestled between my parents' room and my brother's, occupied the front corner of the house. My parents gave me the opportunity to completely transform the space. I was allowed to choose more youthful wallpaper and replace the ubiquitous 1970s green shag carpeting. My decorating choices, even as a second grader, surprisingly stood the test of time. It wasn't until a cataclysmic Category 5 hurricane ravaged our home during my senior year of college that the room's aesthetic underwent any significant change. That sanctuary, my haven throughout childhood and early adulthood, would become my refuge again on the most devastating day of my life, at the age of 31.

Second grade at my new school in Miami started just days before my eighth birthday. Because our moving van had been delayed in a blizzard, all I had to wear were the clothes we brought with us on the plane after spending the holidays in Iowa. I wore Christmas dresses, long pants, and turtlenecks for that first week of school, a wardrobe that was in stark contrast to the T-shirts and shorts my new classmates wore daily. I felt out of place. On the first day at my new school, however, I met Stacey, who would go on to be my best friend to this day. She invited me to eat lunch with her, and I remember telling my mom that Stacey looked like Snow White. Almost immediately, we began riding bikes to each other's homes after school and on the weekends. Having her truly made the adjustment easier.

Over the next few years, I thrived in my new environment. In fourth grade, my teacher, Mr. Dilley, awakened in me a passion for learning that had been smoldering inside me for as long as I had been in school. He was an "outside of the box" teacher with unique ways of bringing out the best in his students. For example, when he was required to implement the state's Florida Studies curriculum, he took us on a three-night camping trip in the Everglades to experience it firsthand.

We slept in tents next to the swamps, sketched sunrises and birds, and listened to talks by park rangers who allowed us to safely touch snakes and alligators. Mr. Dilley was that teacher you remember throughout your life, the one who opened up a whole new world for you. He has since passed, but he is still mentioned on social media by former students who thrived under his teaching and have kept in touch with one another. Some of these people are part of my support system even now, forty-five years later.

Mr. Dilley took a special interest in my academic development and, mid-year, recommended that I be evaluated for the gifted program in our school district. My parents knew little about the program and were surprised one afternoon when I came home from school and announced that I had been tested. I went on to attend the "Cosmos Center," a special academic enrichment program at an alternative elementary school two days a week.

Several of my best friends, including Stacey, were also in the program. We selected classes based on our unique interests, including creative writing, model rocketry, photography, and even gem cutting. The friends I made in this program would stick with me throughout junior high and high school, as we continued to be in each other's classes and drawn to the same academically-based activities. I suppose we were kind of a nerdy group, but that never bothered any of us.

My teen years were full of happiness and stability for our family. Although my mom kept asking my dad when we would be transferred back to Chicago as originally promised, the rest of us loved living in Miami. The truth is, I think she did too. The culture had officially worn off on all of us. We were fully entrenched in Florida living, and my sweet, charismatic dad was progressing up the corporate ladder at work.

My mom did not work outside the home; rather, she was a constant school and community volunteer. She stayed home with my brother and me, who were four years apart in school. My rules growing up were anchored in my parents' Midwestern values and were a bit more restrictive than those of my classmates. I can still hear my mom saying the words, "Nothing good ever happens after midnight." Ironic, given the tragedy that would happen to me in broad daylight shortly after becoming a mother myself.

My parents sensed the changing landscape of Miami, and the increase in crime that accompanied it, long before I did, and enforced strict curfews. To me, and I surmise most of the kids in our neighborhood, Miami felt safe and secure. Life was insular and predictable. As far as we knew, monsters never showed themselves in our community, especially during daylight hours.

My friends and I attended Palmetto Senior High, the neighborhood public school that happened to have a wide variety of excellent academic programs and extracurricular activities. Our community was not very transient. The students in the halls were all familiar year after year. Looking back at my childhood in Miami, I often joke that there must have been something special in the water in our little corner of the city.

Amazon founder Jeff Bezos, Surgeon General of the United States Vivek Murthy, numerous high-profile business people, filmmakers, and famous attorneys all went to high school at Palmetto. The impressive collection of alumni from this Miami public school also includes the newest United States Supreme Court Justice Ketanji Brown Jackson, whom I am proud to say was a mentor and a friend of mine on the high school debate team. I am fortunate that my neighborhood high school surrounded me with so many outstanding classmates and teachers. I know I would not be where I am today without that supportive foundation.

At the end of junior high, Stacey and I decided that the debate team would be our main activity in high school. After all, maybe we would want to be attorneys or politicians when we grew up. Taking a class that taught organized arguing seemed like a good place to start. We loved the thought of being debate partners on a legendary high school team that consistently ranked among the best in the country. If we got good enough, we realized that we could travel to national tournaments on the weekends. We relished the idea of the freedom and academic challenge our new activity could provide us.

Once in high school, the kids on the debate team became like a second family. After the first semester, Stacey and I began traveling nationwide. We met incredible students from around the country at national tournaments. These debaters from other states became some of our closest friends, especially since we hung out with them on the weekends more than we did with our schoolmates in Miami. Debate provided a low-risk social life and a way for us to see the country, while giving us the needed skills and accomplishments to list on our college applications. It turns out that choosing to be on the debate team was one of the best decisions I have ever made, and what I learned from the experience still influences me to this day.

At the start of high school, I zeroed in on attending the University of Virginia (UVA) for college. I was sure I wanted to go to an out-of-state university and experience living outside my comfortable Miami bubble. It didn't hurt that the university had a stellar reputation for academics and a beautiful campus. What was most appealing to me, however, was the chance to study creative writing, American government, and international relations at this incredible school.

Alumni Edgar Allen Poe and William Faulkner were notable English students, and three US presidents were deeply involved in the university's founding. President Woodrow Wilson had also been a scholar at UVA, and from what I had studied about his administration and approach to diplomacy in my high school civics classes, I knew I wanted to be a changemaker one day on Capitol Hill.

I worked extremely hard to make my dream of attending UVA a reality, including promising my parents in tenth grade that I would get an after-school job to help offset some of the cost. Shortly after I turned sixteen, the director of an SAT prep company in my area hired Stacey and me as employees. Any day we were not traveling with the debate team, you could find us working in the office until at least 8 p.m.

This job of tutoring students and doing administrative tasks became another part of my social life, just like the debate team. It was a safe space where I could have some low-stress extracurricular fun while advancing my future goals. Nothing about my life was ever very spontaneous or risky.

The spring of my senior year of high school was probably the happiest time of my young life. In April, college acceptance letters rolled in, and in early May, I learned that I had qualified to compete at the National Championship for Speech and Debate in Philadelphia, PA. It was the triumphant culmination of countless years of self-discipline, intense studying, and sacrificing most of my weekends and summers to compete on behalf of my high school debate team. Life was good, and my future seemed bright.

Also in April, I traveled outside the US for the first time. Back in the fall, my parents had agreed to pay for me to go on the senior class spring break trip to Europe as a graduation gift. When I heard about the trip at the start of the school year, I became excited about the prospect of traveling just for fun, with no tournaments or competitions involved. None of my debate friends signed up for the trip.

However, my high school boyfriend was going, along with about two dozen other people I knew and liked from classes over the years. It would be fun to make travel memories with a different group of people. I remain eternally grateful to my mom and dad for gifting me with this life-changing experience.

Everything in my childhood had prepared me for a bright and predictable future, or so I believed. I had worked hard, planned carefully, and expected life to unfold along the straight path I envisioned. But life has a way of shifting beneath your feet without warning, quietly reminding you that tragedy can touch us all.

2

Detours and Destiny

IT WAS AT THIS point in my life, however, that I realized the truth behind the saying, "Man makes plans, and God laughs."

My trip to Europe was incredible, just not in the way I thought it would be. The weeks before departure were rough. My high school boyfriend broke up with me shortly before the trip, and I was in hot water with my debate coach for missing a crucial state tournament while on my overseas adventure.

On a positive note, however, during the trip I got reacquainted with many of my old childhood friends and became obsessed with traveling abroad and experiencing other cultures. Both later became a large part of my healing journey. Much to my surprise, though, the best souvenir I brought back with me from that trip was an intense friendship with an extremely cute and popular lacrosse player. I can confidently say that he probably never would have even noticed me at school if I hadn't traveled abroad with this group. I am delighted to say that this great guy would become my husband almost a decade later.

After returning home from the trip, I went to the prom, kept working at my after-school job, and daydreamed about my graduation that was now just a few short weeks away. Everything about my future was on track. I made a photo collage of pictures from that spring that I intended to take to college and hang in my dorm room. When my mom saw it, she enthusiastically remarked about how fantastic it was that all of my dreams seemed to be coming true. In hindsight, her words are haunting now. Just one week later, the day before I was supposed to head to the national speech and debate tournament in Philadelphia, my life changed forever.

On May 23, 1989, Stacey and I spent the day together at school, skipping our individual classes to practice for the upcoming tournament. She stayed at school a little longer than I did that afternoon, and so I had to get a different ride to work that day. This was an extremely uncommon thing for me to do since we were always joined at the hip. That simple choice to catch a ride with someone else came with devastating consequences. In a bizarre twist of events, the friend who was driving me to work lost control of the steering wheel while driving down a double S-curving road not far from my church. The car slammed into a tree head-on and crumpled in half.

Fortunately, the driver and our two other friends got out without being severely injured. In contrast, I suffered multiple near-fatal injuries and was airlifted to the trauma center at Jackson Memorial Hospital, located almost an hour away in downtown Miami. I still have, in a box deep inside my closet, the pictures that the Miami-Dade Vehicular Homicide Unit took of the wreckage. No one who was at the scene after the crash expected me to survive.

While all this was unfolding and I was travelling by helicopter to the trauma center, my unsuspecting parents were out celebrating their wedding anniversary. Intending to be home that night to help me pack for my big trip to Philadelphia, they sweetly decided to go out to lunch rather than dinner. They always put us first, and that day was no exception.

When my mom came home that afternoon and heard the garbled message from the trauma center on the answering machine, she was confused. She didn't understand why a hospital so far away from where we lived was calling the house about me since I was supposed to be at work. In fact, it was so out of context, she thought it might be a wrong number. However, the next call on the answering machine was from my boss, wondering why I had not shown up yet.

While my mom tried to make sense of the two messages, Stacey's mom and little sister Randi showed up at our house and started banging frantically on the front door. Stacey's mom was my emergency contact at the high school, and the police had called her in hopes of locating my parents in this era before cell phones.

She filled my mom in with whatever information she had pieced together from the police and drove her to the hospital downtown. My mom was so sickened by the news that she grabbed a wastebasket from our house and repeatedly vomited into it on the way to Jackson Memorial Hospital, Miami's large research hospital and a place none of us had ever been to before.

I would go on to spend about a month in the hospital, including five days in ICU, in a coma on life support. My parents learned that the pastor from our church, whom I had known since second grade, had heard the crash from inside his office and ran over to pray over the victim, not knowing it was me. I am thankful for those prayers in the midst of the emergent chaos.

When I arrived unconscious at the trauma center that day, I had a severe closed-head injury with brain shearing, broken orbital and facial bones, a broken pelvis on both sides, cracked spinal vertebrae, and a nearly severed left arm dangling by a flap of skin below the elbow. I was losing blood at an alarming rate.

The trauma surgeon on call happened to be a member of our church congregation. She had no way to know about this connection at the time, since I initially came in as an unidentified person and we had never been introduced at church before. I am absolutely certain that God put her in my direct path to work miracles on my body in those first hours.

Rather than amputation, she took a chance and decided to perform a complex limb reattachment surgery to save my left arm. Thankfully, it was successful. This surgeon will forever be one of my heroes, and I am pleased to report that she is still in my life.

Suffice it to say, I did not make it back to high school to finish the last couple of weeks of classes or attend any senior events. Most notably, I did not attend the national debate finals, which was the most important thing in my life at that time. Stacey and my other team members went on to Philadelphia the morning after the accident without me, not knowing if I would still be alive when they returned.

So much of my identity was wrapped up in academics and related extracurricular activities that it was especially gut-wrenching for me that everything stopped so abruptly. I was unable to go back to school, experience many traditional rites of passage, or say a proper goodbye to the friends and teachers who had influenced my path up to that point. Fortunately, however, I did manage to make it to my high school graduation.

After I regained consciousness in the hospital, that became the goal that pushed me the hardest when I was stuck in a bed, in pain, and terrified of more surgery and physical therapy. Even if I could not walk across the stage, I was determined to be there in person.

I was released from the hospital the afternoon before the ceremony. That night before bed, while attempting to stand on crutches for a brief moment to brush my teeth, I collapsed unconscious on the bathroom floor. After weeks lying in a hospital bed, my body was not used to standing up, and my blood pressure dropped too low. Fortunately, my mom caught my head before it slammed into the tile.

My parents called 9-1-1, and the paramedics who responded wanted to take me back to the hospital in the ambulance. They felt that I may have been discharged prematurely. I fought like a tiger to stay at home, crying and vowing not to return to the hospital ever again. Thank God for my debate skills.

I graduated the next morning at the Miami-Dade Fairgrounds alongside my classmates, most of whom I had been with since arriving in Miami as that nervous little girl back in 1978. It was not at all how I had envisioned closing this chapter just a few months before.

I was in a wheelchair, wearing a makeshift outfit that accommodated my injuries, weighing less than 90 pounds from being tube-fed for most of the previous month, and generally dazed. There was no triumphant march in with my friends to music and banners flying. I simply waited in the eaves with my family, and my dad pushed me across the stage when my name was called.

I remember the bright lights and cheering, but not very much else. Thankfully, I have pictures from the day that show lots of hugs and happy crying with Stacey, other close friends, and former teachers. While my memories of graduation are very fuzzy and mostly artificially summoned with pictures, that day marked the completion of one of my first milestones in adult life. I remember the bittersweet feeling of it all, though, as I was not sure what was in store for me now that I was severely injured. What would become of me and my carefully planned dreams of college and changing the world? In hindsight, I know now that the entire ordeal helped me build the strength and faith I would call upon decades later.

Shortly after graduation, I had to come to terms with the upsetting reality that I was not going to be able to leave for college that fall to start my freshman year at the University of Virginia. This was something I had worked so hard to accomplish for many years, and now I was left wondering if I would ever be able to go. Fortunately, UVA kept my room assignment open in the hopes that I might be able to matriculate in the spring.

That became my new mission, although I knew it was a longshot. If I wanted to make it happen, I had to completely rebuild myself physically and cognitively, and I only had six months to do it. My body was weak, but my motivation was Herculean.

I was placed in aggressive physical, cognitive, and occupational therapy all summer, learning how to walk again and how to use my new, practically robotic, left arm. The only silver lining to my grueling summer of rehabilitation and healing was reconnecting with that cute boy I met on spring break. He happened to be my neighbor, living on the next street over.

His name was Jamie. Although we couldn't officially be more than friends at that time, he walked over to my house most days and helped me with my therapy exercises, provided me with normal teenage conversation, and made me laugh through the tears of rehab. He sat with me while I grieved what happened to me physically and hugged me as I mourned all of the abilities and opportunities I felt that I had lost forever.

Jamie was also there to celebrate with me when I triumphantly left for UVA in January of 1990 to finally begin my college career. After that, for a variety of reasons (including his family's subsequent move to Philadelphia), we unfortunately lost touch. His love and friendship during that difficult time in my life left a deep impression on my heart. I kept a picture of us from Europe on my bulletin board throughout college.

When I finally arrived on the grounds of UVA in January of 1990, I was excited but also overwhelmed with anxiety. I was finally out of my wheelchair, but apprehensive that I may have overestimated my ability to navigate Virginia's hilly terrain and snow. My steps were tentative, and I was more scared than I had anticipated about falling on the ice.

I clung to my dad with tears in my eyes that day he left me in Charlottesville to return home, even though we both knew that it was necessary if I wanted to realize my dream. After the accident, I became completely reliant on my family during the rehabilitation process as they helped me relearn basic life skills. Their patience, love, and sacrifice were unshakable. I rested securely in that knowledge. But now with them living over a thousand miles away, things felt different. In contrast to my naturally competitive and independent nature, I was now much more tentative and filled with doubt.

I prayed day and night that I would not regret my decision to attempt college a mere eight months after the accident. I prayed that I could still be successful academically despite my significant head injury, that I would be able to make lifelong friendships, and ultimately that I would be able to follow my dreams. I leaned hard on God and asked Him to give me strength for this most uncertain journey. Sometimes my severe anxiety made it hard to trust in His faithfulness.

Sorority rush began two days before the start of spring classes that January, and I decided to participate. Both my parents had been in the Greek system in college and had wonderful memories of their affiliations. I reasoned that it would be a great way to make friends, since everyone would be going through the process for the first time, just like me.

I had missed out on all of the initial camaraderie of the freshman experience by starting college late, but rush was something I could do at the same time as my fellow students. The process was surprisingly enjoyable because the sorority girls I met in the beginning would ask me questions about my interests and future plans, not knowing that just a few months prior to meeting them, I was unable to use my left arm or even walk. I felt normal for the first time in a long time.

I ultimately accepted a bid from Pi Beta Phi, a house where I had authentically connected with many of the sisters during the process. Most importantly, it was a place where the members were compassionate when they learned about what had happened to me and saw value in my healing journey. I didn't feel like a late-comer to the college scene but rather someone who was right on time.

My pledge class was full of women who became supportive friends and would go on to be great leaders at UVA and beyond. Sorority life provided me with the opportunity to meet my future roommates and best friends. Today, via social media and occasional visits back to Charlottesville, VA, for reunions, I have reestablished several old relationships that sustain me in my "new" life. I am so thankful. College in general was just as wonderful as I always dreamed it would be. Although it wasn't without some cognitive and physical challenges early on, I ended up thriving at the University.

By the start of my third year at UVA, I decided to switch my major from English to government and foreign affairs. I took a fascinating class on international organizations with a young, passionate professor named Robert Beck and never looked back. That summer,

I did an independent study on political instability in Haiti under his direction and followed that up with a couple of more courses the following fall.

My final class with him in the spring was called World Order. In the course, we formed groups and conducted mock Security Council meetings. I loved every minute of it. By taking this course, I met several lifelong friends and honed my passion for studying diplomacy. This would come to pay dividends later.

I happily graduated from college on May 23, 1993, on the exact anniversary of my car accident just four years earlier. I ended up graduating on time despite missing the entire first semester. The comeback story could not have been scripted any better, as I fought so hard over the years to regain full function of both my body and my mind at what felt like a lightning pace.

I proved to myself that despite how bleak my dreams looked at times, my determination, fueled by hope, had prevailed. My confidence had come back. I was acutely aware, however, that the real credit belonged to God. He carried me through the hard times and subsequently fueled my desire to go out into the world and make a difference for others.

I would start my next journey in the nation's capital.

3

Building a Life

AFTER COLLEGE ENDED IN May, I came home to Miami for the summer for a little rest and relaxation before moving to Washington, DC, for my first "grown-up" job. I was looking forward to a low-stress summer break. My childhood home was destroyed by Hurricane Andrew the previous August, so my family was living in an apartment near downtown. Despite the apartment's access to the beach and proximity to the city's nightlife, I felt out of sorts not coming back to my old neighborhood.

It had been nine months since the storm, and while my family was fortunate to find a safe and dry place to rent while they rebuilt, it didn't feel like home. We had lost most of our most cherished possessions in a Category 5 hurricane. Returning to Miami that summer ended up feeling like the aftermath of the accident all over again. It was that sense of loving someone, something, or someplace so much that when it abruptly ends or is suddenly destroyed, you feel hopelessly lost and aimless.

Without realizing it, I was beginning to learn the bittersweet concept of "befores and afters." In everyone's lives, there are seminal events that demarcate one part of life from another. The accident had been one of those events, and now the hurricane was one too. It's hard when they happen because you have to stop the story you loved and pivot into a new, and often unwanted, chapter.

I am grateful, however, that I had a chance to learn this lesson early on in life. When I was met with tragedy many years later, I was better prepared for the shock of pivoting. In the back of my mind, I knew at some fundamental level that while life may never be the same as before, it can still be good.

One night that June, I ventured out with a couple of people to a bar closer to where I had grown up. While out, I unexpectedly ran into an old friend. It was Jamie, and my heart skipped a beat the moment I saw him. He and I were excited to reconnect, especially since we lost touch after his family moved to Philadelphia and he went off to engineering school in the northeast.

I told him that while I was in college, I had a picture of us in Germany on my bulletin board and that I always hoped I would see him again. He said that he also kept a similar picture of me from the trip in his room in college and had hoped for the same. It turned out that Jamie was going to be in Miami for the whole summer, interning at an engineering firm and house-sitting for our high school physics teacher who was out of the county. That summer, we spent as much time together as we could, falling madly in love.

Come fall, I started a job outside of my field of study in Washington, DC, that I accepted before my college graduation. Jamie returned to college a couple of hours north of Philadelphia to finish his senior year.

I didn't love my original job out of college, but at least it paid the bills and positioned me in the city I had always dreamed of living in. I rationalized to myself that it didn't matter what I was doing for work initially; just being in Washington, DC, was worth it. I wholeheartedly believed that it wouldn't be long before I found work I loved.

One day, I took the day off from my boring job and got lucky while passing out résumés on Capitol Hill. I scored an interview for a job with the Department of Justice's Antitrust Division and quickly accepted a fantastic position as a legal researcher. I would work all week and then excitedly drive the three hours up to see Jamie on Fridays, or he would drive down to see me. I had everything I had prayed for—new friends, a great job, and love.

By Christmas, Jamie and I realized that if we wanted our relationship to grow more serious, we needed to move to the same city after he graduated. His most promising job offer was with an engineering firm in Miami. In anticipation that he may not move to Washington, DC, I had already applied to graduate programs in foreign affairs at universities in a couple of other prospective cities.

My first acceptance letter came from the University of Miami, and the choice to go was a no-brainer. It was the ideal situation because I received a fellowship that paid for my graduate school tuition and living costs, and I loved the opportunities and connections that UM provided. It was a premier school for Latin American studies and had the international intelligence specialization I was searching for. I left the nation's capital to start a new chapter of life in my hometown and have never regretted that decision.

I loved my time in graduate school and living as an adult in Miami. I completed my degree, along with some postgraduate work, in the summer of 1996. With Jamie living close by, it felt like my fairytale was coming true. In early January 1997, Jamie and I married in a very meaningful ceremony at the church my family and I had been going to since I was eight years old. This church, much like my parents' house and the old neighborhood, was a safe space for me.

Unfortunately, it was also the same location where I almost lost my life and my family five years later.

Life during those first years of marriage was sweet. Jamie and I worked hard at our jobs and enjoyed time with friends. Saving to buy a house was our number one priority, so we filled our weekends with free adventures like long bike rides and trips to the beach. Our day-to-day routine was relatively simple, and we found great joy carving out our new identity as a married couple in the city we both knew and loved.

I look back on those years with great reverence. The versions of Jamie and me that existed back then now seem so innocent and almost naïve. We truly believed that if you worked hard, followed the rules, and filled your heart with love, you would be immune to the evil in the world. Oh, how I wish that were true.

About two years into our marriage, Jamie and I got serious about finding a house and were planning to have children. We considered buying homes in many different parts of the city, as it was tempting to think about living closer to the beach or in a vibrant, younger neighborhood close to downtown.

With community safety and good schools at the forefront of our family plan, however, we ultimately returned to our comfort zone and bought a house in the area where we had gone to high school. It made sense since the community was peaceful, safe, and close to church and family.

We stretched ourselves financially and purchased what we thought would be our "forever home." It was a fairly traditional-looking home by Florida standards, with a partial brick façade and large white columns spread across a wide front porch where we placed white wooden rocking chairs. It was painted a happy shade of yellow and sat on land filled with citrus trees. Our slice of suburbia was a literal oasis in metropolitan Miami.

What we loved the most about this property was that it was situated across from an expansive, federally protected nature preserve where developers were prohibited from building in the future. Back then, we liked the idea of having no neighbors directly across the street from us. Our street was the perfect place to raise children, who would hopefully be fortunate enough to make their own childhood memories in this beautiful space.

Eventually, though, I grew to loathe the idea of isolation. It turns out that monsters who operate in the daylight are also drawn to quiet, peaceful neighborhoods, as they make for perfect hunting grounds for unsuspecting mothers and families.

4

Babies and Blessings

A FEW MONTHS AFTER moving into our new house, I found out that I was pregnant with our first child. One of the things that drew Jamie and me together from the start was our shared love of kids and our commitment to someday be loving parents.

Before the pregnancy, however, I suffered with a great deal of anxiety over being able to successfully carry a child due to the pelvic and lower back fractures I sustained in my car accident nearly a decade before. Doctors mentioned in follow-up visits over the years that it might not be possible. I prayed constantly after my injury that someday I would be a mother, through either pregnancy or adoption, and was blessed that I had a partner who prayed for the same.

Luckily, despite the intense morning sickness I experienced in the first trimester, the pregnancy was uneventful. My bones and joints were in constant pain, but I used that discomfort to motivate myself to find meditative spaces in my mind to practice thankfulness and patience.

I filled my weekdays working at Royal Caribbean Cruise Lines' corporate headquarters near downtown Miami, and my weekends resting and preparing for the upcoming birth. My mother told me to relish this season in life, because everything would become much more hectic once the baby arrived.

We did not find out the baby's gender and enjoyed months of walking our neighborhood and sitting on our front porch, lost in speculation about what we would be having. Early in the pregnancy, Stacey's sister Randi got married, and Jamie found a small charm under his chair at the reception. In script pink foil lettering, it said, "It's A Girl," most likely left over from a baby shower at the venue days before. The power of suggestion made us believe deep down that a daughter was our destiny.

We held on to the charm. Mia was born in late September of 1999. After two difficult hours of pushing, my pelvic bones could not take it anymore, and she came into the world via C-section with a very robust cry. The sound of a healthy, screaming baby was music to my ears. So many of my prayers in life centered around becoming a mother. The day of her birth, I truly felt the presence of God in my hospital room.

The moment I looked into Mia's sweet face, I was stunned by the overwhelming love I felt for this tiny soul. She was pure light, and my heart rejoiced that Jamie and I were given the privilege of becoming her parents. My life changed forever when our daughter was born.

Much like what happened after my accident and following Hurricane Andrew, time would be defined again by the concept of before and after. Rather than the split coming as a result of devastating trauma this time, this transition was filled with joy instead of grief. I happily accepted my new role and relished my new name, Mom.

Jamie and I had started going to church more and more after we got married and quickly fell into a group with a few other newlywed couples. Surprisingly, this was a different group of people than either of us had been friends with in high school or that I hung out with in the youth group at the same church growing up. These people would become our "grown-up" friends, special because these were among the first relationships we made as a married couple.

Everyone we met this way was going through the same things we were—working hard, saving money, and planning for a family. We found ourselves almost exclusively socializing with this group, doing Bible studies and celebrating life events together like job promotions, buying homes, and welcoming children into the fold.

Since Jamie and I were the first ones to buy a home, and because it was literally walking distance from the church we all attended, our place became the site of many group dinners, holiday parties, and playdates. I loved having a full house and entertaining.

Household duties, babies, and new friends made me feel like my life had expanded exponentially. In contrast, however, everything we truly needed geographically was now within a few-mile radius of our home. The space that anchored our happiness and presence in Miami was drastically shrinking. And we were content with that.

When Mia was about three months old, I got together with a few other new moms and started a playgroup in the basement of our church that met weekly. I cannot stress enough how important that group became to all of us as we navigated our way through sleepless nights, colicky babies, and the postpartum challenges of being wives and mothers.

Most of us in the group were stay-at-home moms who had college degrees and had worked prior to the birth of our kids. Some of the moms were on their second go-round with infants and toddlers. Having been a type A personality all of my life, I found this group to be a wonderful fit as I adjusted to my less structured and far-from-predictable new role as a mom.

One day, in a sermon, the pastor at our church likened our playgroup to a successful Fortune 500 company, given the way we planned exciting events and recruited new members. We all loved how busy our social schedules were once the group took root and how much time we got to spend together raising our kids while playing and learning. It was great socialization for our little ones, but a true lifesaver from the isolation that can sometimes set in when you are a new parent.

On May 23, 2001, Jamie and I found out we were expecting again. We could not believe how special the timing was. That date on the calendar now marked my parents' wedding anniversary, the anniversary of my near-fatal car accident, my college graduation, and now news of a new soul that was destined to join our family.

Every year, I pause on that date to acknowledge what it has come to represent: the reality of life, loss, and beauty all mixed together in a wild tapestry that defied my plans but led to my dreams. Our bundle of joy would be arriving in February 2002, and we began preparing for him/her with great excitement.

Despite another round of intense morning sickness, the pregnancy was once again uneventful. We decided to find out the gender this time, and although we truly had no preference, we were elated to learn we would be having a son. Our joy was put on pause, however, as just a few days later, the world erupted into chaos with the events of 9/11. In fact, I was driving to take a blood test at my obstetrician's office when I heard the news of the first plane crash into the Twin Towers on talk radio.

By the time I arrived at my appointment, the second plane had hit the towers, and talk of terrorist attacks was dominating the constant news cycle. Everyone was fleeing the office building, so I rushed back to my car, cradling my growing belly and the life inside of it with every step. The main roads in South Miami were jammed with honking cars, filled with panicked people trying to get home. I sped down all of the familiar backstreets to our church, where Mia was anxiously waiting for me in her preschool classroom.

When I arrived, moms and kids were all spinning in the chaos that morning. The moms were visibly afraid but trying not to scare the children. As I grabbed Mia's tiny hand and led her back to the safety of our car, my heart was heavy. In hindsight, that was my first brush with profound evil breaching the secure walls of our everyday life. Right there in the church parking lot, outside her classroom, the world as I knew it shifted.

I prayed for God's protection. News coverage from that day forward turned into a 24-hour cycle that was constantly updating on television. I spent many days during my pregnancy closely following the recovery operations after 9/11, better acquainting myself with information about the Taliban, and praying daily for the capture of Osama Bin Laden.

By education, I am a foreign policy analyst, and this simple fact drove my passion to find out as many details as I could, almost as if it were my job. I watched the news channels every chance I could, between episodes of Elmo and during naptimes. My academic interest in both the masterminds behind the attack and the governments that were involved, however, quickly morphed into urgent, tangible fear for my family's safety.

As my pregnancy progressed, I obsessed about things like anthrax exposure, escape routes if terrorists bombed Miami, and what US military service might look like when my son someday turned eighteen. The world suddenly felt fragile in ways I had never considered before.

Mia's sweetness in the months between 9/11 and Peter's birth grounded me. Having a child and trying to stay hopeful about the world became a comforting buffer during an otherwise frightful season. At preschool, they made care packages for the soldiers and prayed daily for our country. When Mia asked innocent questions about what had happened, who had done the "terrible thing," and if she was safe, it challenged my own concept of faith. How do you explain evil to a preschooler? How do you explain it to anyone?

Mia had seen villains in Disney movies and, while frightened by the images, was assured that we would always protect her. How could I confidently promise that now? Her teachers had a gentle, God-centered approach to calming the children's anxieties, especially in the early days, and I tried to find that rhythm at home as well. *God will shelter us*, was my mantra.

With the constant distractions of caring for my daughter while the world was whirling out of control, my pregnancy seemed to pass by quickly. As the birth grew closer, Mia was sad to leave the safety of her nursery, but fortunately, she transitioned well into her new big girl room. Suddenly, I stopped viewing her as a toddler and saw her as a budding big sister.

Like many other mothers, I felt guilty in the days leading up to our son's birth. I couldn't wait to become a. family of four, but I was scared to disrupt the sacred bond we had made as a family of three. Mia was the center of our world. Just before our son's arrival, my mom explained to me that the love in your heart doesn't divide when you have another baby, but rather multiplies exponentially. I wanted that to be true for my heart, but I wasn't entirely convinced it was possible.

Turns out my mom was right. Peter came peacefully into the world as our early Valentine's Day gift at dawn one February morning. Mia's emergency delivery had proved to everyone that my previously broken pelvic joints were not going to fully cooperate in the birthing process, so Peter was born via planned C-section. One look at his perfect little face and my heart broke open wide, just like I had been promised.

My world was now a delightful swirl of blue and pink, and I felt so lucky and content. I was understandably overwhelmed being the mom of two kids under three, but I remember loving the chaos. My parents only lived about three miles away from us, and I was grateful for their help when I needed it.

Mia was now in preschool three half-days a week, and this was a huge blessing since my husband was continuously putting in sixty to seventy hours a week at the office and often worked late nights and weekends. We were trying to make it as a one-income family, so his job security was of paramount importance. When I think back on those first eight months as a family of four, I recall the intense exhaustion we both felt but remember more the strength we lent to each other and the love that got us through. We knew that children are only little for a moment in time and that someday we would wish for these days back. At the time, we had no idea how painfully true that sentiment would become.

I leaned hard on my playgroup friends during this season for advice on everything from potty training to what minivan I should get. Mia, now a verbally precocious three-year-old, loved being with other kids, so we were always meeting up at parks or having people over to the house.

During that time, the bonds of friendship within the playgroup grew stronger, and so did my faith. I wanted to be the best mother that I could for my son and daughter. I felt so grateful that I had the opportunity to nurture and protect their tiny hearts. I was going to playgroup every week, planned activities like scrapbooking and movie nights on the weekends, and had even added a Bible study that came with an insane amount of homework.

Adding in Sunday worship and preschool pickups and drop-offs, I was on the grounds of my church five or six days a week. With the exception of my college years, I had been attending there since I was eight years old, and the church at this point felt like an extension of my own home.

I suppose that's what makes what happened next so hard to reconcile in my head.

5

The Last Ordinary Day

OCTOBER 16, 2002, STARTED out like a typical day in our house. Jamie went off to work, I fed and dressed the kids, and then Peter and I went to drop Mia off at preschool. She loved going to school three half-days a week, even though they were short. That day, I had an unusually busy morning of errands planned for Peter and me.

Before we left home, I hastily threw together a diaper bag and grabbed my phone, keys, and wallet. In my rush, however, I absent-mindedly left Peter's diaper bag on the floor. Within minutes, we dropped off Mia in her classroom, briefly chatted with friends, and then went on our way. In three hours, we would be back for pick-up, lunch, and naps.

Unfortunately, our errands took much longer than expected that morning, and I ended up driving straight back to the church instead to pick up Mia at noon. There was no time for the original plan, which was to stop by the house to change Peter's extremely wet diaper and give him a quick bottle. His constant cries over the last hour signaled he was miserable and overdue for both.

When I got to the church, I parked along the back wall of the parking lot, across from the playground, and close to Mia's class-room. Most days, I parked in one of the two busy side lots to socialize with some of my mom friends who were hanging out in their cars before the official release time. On this day, however, my tardiness made me prioritize convenience, and I chose to park in the rear of the school, where there were only a few other vehicles. I rarely, if ever, parked there. It didn't seem like a big deal to me at the time, though, as my plan was to get in and out of the parking lot as fast as possible.

Mia and her teacher greeted us with big smiles as we hurriedly entered the classroom. Mia had accomplished something new at school that day and couldn't wait to tell us all about it. A trip to the church bookstore for a lollipop seemed like a nice way to celebrate the great day she was having.

We slowed our pace down a bit and spent time browsing through books and picking out just the right flavor of candy. After about 10 minutes, we decided to head back to the van, a little bit off our usual schedule. The parking lot was pretty much empty since all of the families who attended the half-day program were done with pick up.

Even with no traffic, I instinctively held Mia's hand tightly as we walked to the car, Peter securely resting on my hip. Five more minutes and we would be back home. When we arrived at the van, the door slid open, and Mia jumped inside. We had just purchased the minivan, and she loved the "magic" doors and all of the interior space to play around.

We had recently taken the new car to Disney World and separated the kids' car seats, so they each had their own row. While I started to buckle Peter into his car seat, which was located right behind me on the driver's side, Mia explained that she was the big sister and no longer needed my help. Today, she would be buckling herself into her seat in the back row on the passenger side. I chuckled at her independence just as my good friend Tina drove up alongside me.

Tina always knew how to make me laugh, and spending even a few minutes with her brightened my day. On this afternoon, we bantered a bit about what we were making for dinner and talked about plans for our upcoming playgroup scrapbooking night. The kids grew restless while I stood outside the van, gabbing.

When Tina and I were done talking, she rolled up her car window and slowly drove away. In an especially good mood, I found myself alone for a few seconds, fumbling with my key fob and preparing to shut the "magic" sliding door. In my mind, I can still see the taillights of Tina's car leaving the church as the ambush began. My body, my family, and my future would be forever changed by the evil that found us in that moment.

Just as I finished locking Peter's car seat buckle in place and began to jump into the van, I heard an intense rustling sound behind me. I thought it was the sound of squirrels or other small animals wrestling in the excessive vegetation that dominated most of the parking lot's edges. Within seconds, however, I experienced an intense and disabling pain on the top of my head. It felt like a brick had fallen straight out of the sky and cracked my skull.

Dazed and extremely confused, I tried to steady myself and looked straight forward into the van. Immediately, I saw the pure terror in Mia's face as she began to scream. The piercing sound of her cries was then accompanied by the feeling of two large hands grabbing me and a cold metal blade being drawn across my neck. In the chaos of those ensuing moments, my world felt like it was hurling out of control as excruciating pain and abject fear collided.

A man began to yell, "Get in the car bitch! If you don't want your babies to die, get in the car." Then his low, but manic, voice shouted into my ear words that are seared into my brain forever, "Do you believe in God?" Without even thinking, I cried out to the heavens and told the stranger behind me, "Yes." In response, my assailant said, "Good, then you will forgive me for what I am going to do to you and to your two kids." My heart sank. This person did not want to steal my van or my wallet. He had something else planned for all of us, and I instantly sensed that the plan could be fatal.

His tight grip on my body from behind physically overwhelmed me. I fought to get free, but his large size and the presence of the knife made that impossible. Before he stripped the keys out of my hand and violently shoved my body into the van, he had one important instruction. "Do not make eye contact with me. If you do, I will kill you and your children without thinking twice." He bizarrely stated that what he was about to do to us was punishable by life in prison and that if we could identify him, we were better off to him dead.

Despite his terrifying warning, Mia continued to scream for help and fought to escape. As our assailant got into the vehicle and was preparing to shut the sliding door behind him, she made a very brave attempt to jump out. He forcibly grabbed Mia and roughly threw her tiny body into the back row.

It tore my heart to pieces to hear her cries immediately shift from ones of confusion and fear to ones borne out of physical pain. As her mom, I just wanted to protect and comfort her, wrap her in my arms, and assure her everything was going to be alright. Unfortunately, I was growing more convinced that it wouldn't be.

With the van doors finally shut, I was ordered to get into the passenger seat with my eyes tightly shut. The man started the ignition and turned the volume on the radio all the way up to muffle our cries. He demanded my wallet right away, not to steal it from me but to read my driver's license. He was desperate to see my address and know my name. He explained that he had just been released from prison and needed money and whatever guns I had access to.

I tried telling him that we had neither cash nor weapons, which was the truth. I had always been afraid of guns, and Jamie had no desire to have them with little kids in the house. Our abductor paid no attention to what I was saying and ripped the license out of my wallet. In a very macabre way, he started chuckling when he saw that we lived right around the corner. "It's my lucky day. Let's go home, babe!" he laughed. With that, he threw the van into drive and sped out of the lot.

My breaking heart tried to hold on tight to whatever shred of hope it could find. My mind was racing through scenarios, and I rationalized that someone might have witnessed the original altercation or heard our screams. Maybe someone at the preschool or working on the grounds of the church heard the van wheels squeal as we left the parking lot or noticed the deafening music coming from inside the vehicle. There were plenty of students and teachers still at the school for the afternoon session, and I was hopeful that someone would send help immediately.

Spoiler: Help did not come.

Once we arrived in my neighborhood, I thought a neighbor might notice something was wrong. Unfortunately, living across the street from the peaceful nature preserve we loved so much became a liability at this stage of my ordeal. We had no houses across from us, and, in fact, there were only three other houses on the entire street.

On that hot afternoon, no one was in their yards to see or hear us as we entered the neighborhood speeding erratically. No one was there when we drove away moments later, either, after the perpetrator realized that I was telling the truth about having no guns or money. When I left my little happy yellow house this time, I did it with the visceral fear that we may never return.

6

Trapped and Terrorized

AS WE REACHED THE stop sign at the end of my street, the stranger locked the doors and pulled down his navy blue athletic shorts. At knifepoint, he commanded me to get on my knees between the two front seats. He called Mia up to the front of the van and directed her to sit in the passenger seat.

I was ordered to start performing oral sex on him as he continuously struck me on the back of the head. Most of the time, he hit me with the handle of the knife that he used to disable me at the start. Sometimes, however, he struck me with his fist. The blows were painful.

Both of my children were crying as loudly as I had ever heard them. Fear filled the inside of the van, and it became hard to think about anything except basic survival. I tried to find some strength between my gasps for air and began thinking like the prey I had become. If I could not escape, then I had to endure. If I could not endure, then my children would not survive. We had to outsmart our predator.

Strangely, the predator liked to talk. At first, he barked orders like "close your eyes," "stop crying," "suck harder," "shut those kids up." Then, he started asking questions, "What are their names?" "Do you love your husband?" "What's his name?" "Where is your phone?" "How long until anyone notices you're gone?" The man actually wanted answers, and so he repeated the questions.

With the blade pressed into my neck, he demanded that I answer him in between the chokes of the oral assault. I told him my children's names, which were so difficult to speak out loud. The anonymity that I wanted them to have in his eyes was now gone. I sobbed when I told him that I loved Jamie very much, and that I knew that my husband loved me and our children in return. The man grumbled expletives under his breath and then responded with glee. "Well, that's all over now, you dirty, cheating whore. No one will love you after this but me."

With respect to my cell phone, I told him that I left it at home in the diaper bag so that he would not worry about me trying to call for help. In the moment, I honestly did not remember picking it up when I headed out that morning for errands. I thought that information would calm him down, but it had the opposite effect. He violently berated me for being so careless.

His words landed with intention. He wanted me broken, ashamed, and convinced that what was happening was my fault. He said I was a terrible mother, too distracted and absentminded to protect my kids. I secretly harbored hope, however, that if my phone was somehow inside the vehicle, the ringer was off, so he wouldn't think I lied to him intentionally. His rage was more frightening than anything I had ever experienced before.

Although phones in 2002 were extremely basic and did not have internet capabilities as they do now, I hoped that maybe there was some way to track mine if we never came back. When the man became distressed and demanded to know when people would notice me missing, I told him the truth about our daily routine. I explained that my mom came over most days in the late afternoon to visit with the children while I made dinner, and that my husband usually arrived home around seven.

He seemed pleased with my answers. "That leaves plenty of time for us, sweetheart," he cooed mockingly. "Now back on your knees, bitch." He then looked at Mia and directly asked her, "What did your mother do to make God hate your family so much?" She started to cry harder.

In preschool and at home, especially after 9/11, she had learned about God's unfailing and protective love that we all promised would keep her safe. I sensed in that moment that whatever sense of safety she had known was now gone as I listened to her sob uncontrollably. I tried to collect myself the best I could.

At this point, I knew by silently counting the turns we made leaving our neighborhood that we were about to get onto Old Cutler Road. This road is one of the prettiest and most historic in all of Miami-Dade County, lined with beautiful canopies of trees and tropical vegetation. It runs south and east, not far from Biscayne Bay.

In the pit of my stomach, I could not reconcile the beauty of this oft-travelled road with where we might be headed or with what could be waiting for us at the end of it. The contrast felt cruel, as if the world itself were indifferent to what was unfolding inside the van.

My abductor was smart. He knew it was a local two-lane road where no one would be able to pull up alongside us and see into the van or realize that there was an unbuckled three-year-old in the front seat. Even if someone did get that close, no one would ever suspect that it could be tied to horrific evil within the quaint community. I knew that this was what he was thinking because he talked me through his logic. Constant chatter.

Eventually, Old Cutler Road came to an end deep in southern Miami-Dade County. I grew up south of the city of Miami, in the safety of the suburbs, but the roads in the extreme ends of the county were still a bit mysterious to me. Our abductor, however, zigged in and out of the backroads like he knew them well.

By the time we reached the edge of familiarity, I understood something with terrifying clarity: there was nowhere left to run. The well-kept roads fell away behind us, replaced by stretches of isolation where no one could see us, hear us, or intervene. Whatever was going to happen next would happen far from help, far from home, and entirely beyond my control.

After a little bit of time driving out in unfamiliar territory, I could tell from our speed that we had gotten off local roads and slipped onto the southernmost extension of the Florida Turnpike for a moment. My heart felt a bit of relief since this meant maybe someone would see us now. If anyone had called 9-1-1 after we left the church parking lot or our house, maybe the police would pull us over. Perhaps someone driving next to us would notice Mia looking out of the passenger side window, unrestrained and still crying. Hope, even when it is irrational, can feel like oxygen.

Homestead is the name of the city at the end of the turnpike. It's much more developed now, but in the early 2000s, it was still fairly remote and happened to be the best place to shop and refuel at the end of the peninsula before heading down to the Florida Keys. I recognized the vintage signs for fruit stands and tourist attractions that had been there for decades. They reminded me of pleasant childhood adventures.

Whether it was en route to a hike with my fourth-grade class in the Everglades or driving to Stacey's vacation house in the Keys for some relaxation, Homestead signaled to me an end to the crowds of suburban Miami and a gateway to something fun. How perverse that these landmarks now seemed poised to mark where my family, as I knew it, died.

The last symbol of civilization I saw before heading into the marshy area of the swamp was the city's name on a large, white tower near the newly reconfigured Homestead Motorsports Complex. At some point, I had managed to lift my head out of my abuser's lap long enough to sneak a peek at it through the van window as we made a turn to the East.

As we drove, the tower sadly faded into the distance, and my children and I were driven into total isolation. With that landmark went the last illusion that we were still connected to the outside world. I had tried my best since the moment he took us in the church parking lot to stay calm for my kids and do everything I could to keep my perpetrator as even-tempered as possible.

When I realized that we were entering no-man's-land, however, a feeling of unforgettable terror cut through my heart. I knew at that moment that no one would be coming to save us and that it was up to me to keep my family alive. I have never, ever felt so desperate or powerless.

7

Nowhere to Run

IN 1947, WRITER MARJORY Stoneman Douglas aptly referred to the Everglades National Park as the "river of grass," due to the slow flow of water through its subtropical prairieland. The Everglades cover 1.5 million acres of territory in the southern half of Florida. Dotted with marshes and hardwood hammocks, this unique ecosystem is both beautiful and predatory.

Hundreds of species of birds call the Everglades home. Great Blue Herons, Snowy Egrets, and the colorful Roseate Spoonbill can often be seen wading in the brackish estuaries and tall sawgrass. In contrast to their peaceful beauty, many natural predators also live in the subtropical marshlands. Florida panthers, venomous snakes, as well as alligators and crocodiles, are common residents that remind visitors of the raw, untamed spirit of the land.

The Everglades was something that had always fascinated me. I grew up taking family day trips into the national park and visiting with its wild inhabitants. One of my best childhood memories was the three-day overnight field trip I took there with Mr. Dilley's 4th-grade class. On the day we were abducted, however, the Everglades instantly transformed from a tourist destination that captured the essence of nature's dichotomy into a backdrop where only one predator was in control.

While driving us several miles out into the swamp on vacant access roads, the kidnapper spoke directly to my daughter and me about what might happen to us if we attempted to escape the van. He made sure that my daughter knew that if she did anything to stop what he was going to do to me, she would die.

He graphically described how he would sink our vehicle into the canal next to where we ultimately parked. In exquisite detail, like he was reading a horror story to a small child, he described how the gators would tear all of our bodies apart and that no one would ever find us. She promised him that she would behave and not cause any trouble. I agreed to the same. My son just kept crying, and the man told me that if I couldn't shut him up, "the boy" would be the first to die. I wasn't sure how much more fear my heart could hold.

Immediately after making threats that he would kill us, my daughter was ordered to leave the passenger seat so that I could recline the seat and lie there for him. I was instructed to take off all of my clothes so that he could inspect every inch of my body. My daughter took her place beside him as he gave a profanity-laced commentary on my naked form.

I vividly remember the intense heat inside the van. My gas tank was less than half full when he took us from the church, so he was careful to shut off the air conditioning while driving so that we wouldn't have to stop to refuel at a gas station. October is still well within hurricane season in Florida, and the outside temperatures hover in the high eighties and nineties with extreme humidity.

When he parked the van in the Everglades, it sat baking in the sun, and the temperature inside became unbearable, easily over one hundred degrees. The same landscape that had once felt wild but wondrous to me now pressed in on us, indifferent and unforgiving.

Once he was satisfied with his inspection of my body, he pulled his shorts all the way down and climbed on top of me.

The sweat that dripped from his body onto my skin burned like acid, and I cried loudly as I felt the intense pain of him entering me. As he began the rape, my worst fears as both a woman and a mom began to play out in front of my children in Technicolor. The rapist was in no hurry to complete the assault.

Between thrusts and during brief breaks, he droned on about what his motivation was for taking us. The man said he had been raised by a drug addicted, prostitute mother who had no idea who his father was. He grew up on the streets of inner-city Miami with no one to look out for him, so he dropped out of school and turned to crime to survive. His life had been so horribly violent from the start that he grew to hate people who grew up in the suburbs and had the life that he didn't.

Feeling that God had cursed him from the start, he developed a specific hatred for church-going moms whom he perceived to be carefree and entitled. Moms like me, he explained, who were unfairly spared the ugliness of life and blessed by a hypocritical God who didn't truly love everyone equally.

It was his stated mission that day to turn me into the dirty whore his mother was and create enough suffering through his depravity that my children's lives would be ruined forever, just like his. Not only did he want to destroy me physically, but he wanted to take away the innate sense of love and security my children felt. He wanted them to believe God had abandoned them too.

As the time dragged on, the heat inside the van intensified. The pain of the repeated assaults increased as he became more aggressive. My rapist bragged that he had done this to several women in the past and teased that he would never be caught. He taunted me, saying that there was no way that a simple housewife like me could ever outsmart him.

He boasted that he was an expert criminal and never left any evidence behind, despite the multiple violent rapes he committed. In fact, he was proud to report that he had just abducted a woman at a different Presbyterian preschool a few miles away from mine, a couple of weeks earlier, and that the abduction had not even made the news. He likened himself to the Washington, DC sniper—a criminal who was making national headlines at the time—by evading capture.

At this point in the assault, my son began to get fussy and cried again after briefly passing out from hunger, heat, and exhaustion. The stranger screamed at me to reach back and hold my baby's hand to calm him down. I was also ordered to look directly into my son's eyes so that for the rest of my life, his beautiful eyes would trigger memories of the brutality of my rape. This act, he assured me, would make me his prisoner forever. After that bold and disgusting proclamation, his attack on me sped up, and he told me he was nearing completion.

He had explicit instructions about what I was to do with the flood of DNA that was about to be released. He ordered me to swallow it all, instructing me not to spill or throw up a single drop, otherwise he would kill me. He mused out loud, like he was making plans with a friend, that if I followed his instructions, there would be no way for law enforcement to identify him, and he would "win" again.

Abruptly, he withdrew himself from inside my body, held the knife blade to my neck, and put himself in my mouth. I did as instructed, although my body's instinct was to gag and fight what he commanded me to do. I kept telling myself that I had to endure whatever torture was happening to save my children's lives.

Somehow, I found the strength inside of me to comply with his demands, and I feigned delight as I swallowed the evidence. This seemed to pacify him momentarily, and I was grateful for the short pause in the chaos. It was a small victory, but any respite from the violence sparked hope in me that we might survive.

8

The Shift

UP UNTIL THIS POINT, everything I had done was instinctual—reactive, primal, driven by terror and the singular goal of keeping my children alive. But somewhere in the stillness that followed, after the worst violations had already occurred, something inside me shifted. The man believed he had erased his evidence, broken my will, and secured complete control. What he did not realize was that survival had awakened a different part of me. Fear was no longer the loudest voice in my mind: strategy was.

When the initial rape was over, he quickly regained his focus. The van was hot and steamy from all of the frenetic activity, so he cracked the windows for a bit of relief. I have never been so happy to breathe fresh air, air not tainted with the putrid stench of my abuser.

He said that he still needed to get money from me and wanted to take me to a bank. He had seen a debit card inside my wallet. As he put the car in drive, I began to feel alive again. I desperately needed a reason for him to take us back to civilization, and going to a bank was the perfect excuse to leave the swamp. He eventually drove the van out of the Everglades and back to Homestead, stopping for a moment on the edge of a bank parking lot to figure out his plan.

First, he mumbled that I needed to put my shirt on so that I could conduct business with the teller and gruffly threw the Tinkerbell T-shirt I had been wearing at me. As I slipped the shirt over my head, I remembered how sweetly Mia had asked me to wear it the previous night. It was a souvenir she had picked out for me at Disney the week before, a reminder of happy times.

The next few moments would be anything but happy as we were about to carry out the next step of our abductor's plan. He explained to me that we were going to try to clear out my checking and savings accounts by going through the drive-up teller lane.

I was to take his place in the driver's seat, while he went to the rear of the van and held the knife to my daughter to keep her from screaming and me from alerting anyone. I prayed silently as I drove up to the bank window, pleading with God to give us the chance to escape or at least for someone to notice we were in danger.

When it was my turn in line, I pulled up and put my debit card into the tube provided. I then sent the tube from my car over to the smiling teller. She greeted me politely and asked what kind of transaction she could assist me with. I calmly explained that I needed to withdraw all of the money from my accounts in cash, if possible.

I did not want to do anything rash out of fear for my kids, but I was hoping that the teller would at least notice the bruising on my puffy, tear-stained face and sense that we were in trouble. I hoped she could see the crazed man in the back of the vehicle with a knife on my daughter and press a silent alarm for help. I just knew this was going to be how we would be rescued. Game over.

Tragically, the teller did not recognize the fear or urgency in my eyes and simply informed me that the daily limit for cash withdrawals was $400. She asked if there was anything else she could help me with, and I sighed, "No." I felt so defeated and hopeless after an afternoon spent praying for a miracle.

Just like back at the church and in my neighborhood, help seemed so close but, at the same time, completely out of reach. I drove away as instructed and returned to the edge of the parking lot, where the strange man got back into the driver's seat.

After he was in control again, he demanded both the cash and the receipt. When he saw that there were funds left in the checking account, he grew frantic to access the money. He started scheming out loud. I tried to be as clever as possible and gently suggested that maybe, because the bank we had just left was not my personal bank, he should drive me back to my neighborhood and let me try to withdraw money from the branch I had been banking at for years. He liked that idea and agreed that it was what we should do. I couldn't believe he was going to drive me closer to home. Maybe I would have another chance to signal for help.

My tiny burst of hope was extinguished, however, when his anger towards me started to rise to the surface again. He yelled at me and said I was stupid to think that our time together in South Miami-Dade was over. We would get the money later, maybe, but first, he had other plans. The next couple of hours went by in a blur, every minute seeming like a lifetime of uncertainty and terror.

He continued talking to me about his life and about the whore he was determined to make me into. At one point, he stopped the van near a seemingly abandoned citrus processing plant. Something changed between us once we were settled into place, obscured by tropical overgrowth at the location.

Things grew more conversational between us here, less threatening and more like role play, though no less dangerous. Although the tension in the air abated a little from our time in the Everglades, the calm conversation grew macabre very quickly. He saw us as a couple now, a family.

At the beginning of the crime, after we went to my house, he yanked the wedding rings off my fingers and rubbed them on his genitals, erotically describing the sensation. Now, he produced them in his hands and asked me to be his wife. He started to kiss me forcefully and passionately, disgustingly purring romantic phrases into my ears like we were lovers.

He told me that he wanted the children to see how much he loved me and how he would be a much better husband and father than Jamie was. My daughter began to cry again, wondering what he had done to her father and why he was replacing him. The psychological torture he was subjecting everyone to, especially my daughter, was mind-blowing. I prayed so hard for Jamie to be okay and for my children's minds to be protected from the evil they were being exposed to.

When he wanted to have our own marriage ceremony in the van, to become married in the eyes of my kids, I knew I couldn't refuse him. We said short vows while my daughter and son wept in the background. Right after the ceremony, he exclaimed that we had to demonstrate our love in front of the children.

To please my rapist, I went overboard expressing my desire for him as my children listened from just feet away. In the back of my mind, I thought that if I could play the "good wife," he might keep us alive. Our abductor and I kissed deeply and held each other close as he explained that it was time to consummate our relationship.

He told the children to watch us make love as a sign before God that we were a "proper" family now, together forever. It took every shred of strength in my body not to throw up the biological evidence when he forced me to swallow it again. The knife on the dashboard, however, served as a good motivator.

Instead of being painted as a whore this time, my compliance was celebrated as proof that I wanted it to happen. I'm sure it was confusing to the kids why I seemed so happy to be "married" to the man who was constantly threatening to kill us. Although the mechanics of the rape were less physically distressing this time, the psychological pain I experienced was unrivaled.

Turning my sexual assault into a religious covenant before God was more than my mind could handle. I felt repulsed by myself, deep down in my soul. It all felt so filthy and blasphemous. I felt like I was actually morphing into the whore my rapist was hoping to turn me into. I was worried that I was truly too dirty to be loved anymore: by my kids, my husband, or my God.

I had played along; I made promises of love to an evil man and didn't fight this time as he penetrated my body. I didn't want any of it, but he was convinced I did. Cerebrally, I knew that my actions were a ruse to keep us alive, but psychologically, he had poisoned my spirit.

Each time I was raped on October 16th was painful and terrifying. While the rapes differed in location, they never deviated in intent. He was determined to humiliate me and make me as unclean in the eyes of God as possible. His constant need to talk about himself and his masculine supremacy, both as a successful criminal and as a sexual creature, was relentless.

This was especially true with the next assault, as I sensed the rosy glow of our "marriage" starting to wear off. While the honeymoon period was extremely short-lived, I was grateful that it gave me a much-needed breather and allowed me to regain some physical strength during brief moments of respite.

Before he took my body this time, the loving demeanor that I hoped would persist began to transform back into rage. He now saw himself as the possessive and abusive husband I needed, a man who was now empowered through a so-called "biblical" marriage to dominate and control me.

Still out in South Dade, about forty minutes from our original abduction spot at the church, he kept us on the geographic fringes of the county. We were back into swampy territory now, characterized by tall grasses and the kind of isolation that kept us terrified. He pulled off the road to rape me here. He was my "husband," and I had an obligation to satisfy him now, whenever he wanted.

He started to hit me again and scream despicable things at me, while assaulting my body. The volume on the radio was, again, all the way up, with the windows tightly closed to muffle the cries of everyone in the van. I was exhausted down to my bones, but he apparently still felt like Superman, with what seemed like an unending amount of both adrenaline and testosterone inside of his veins. The rape finished as the other two had, with me holding my son's hand while being forced to destroy the evidence.

After this assault was complete, he took a few minutes to threaten us some more. He reminded all of us that death was probably the only way we could escape from him. Each time this weird pattern played out, I honestly believed in my heart that I was going to die. One wrong move or word from my mouth would get us all killed.

The pressure on me to play this repetitive game of survival was agonizing. For a few fleeting moments at this point, death seemed like the easy way out. I was exhausted from hours of screaming and crying, I was hungry and dehydrated, and on a primal level, I wanted nothing more than to just lie down and stop fighting.

But this battle was not about me. This fight was to save the lives of the two innocent, beautiful souls trapped in that van with me. There was no possible way I could abandon the mission after promising them, from the day they were born, that I would love and protect them every second of their lives.

When my son and daughter were born, I knew from the moment that I held them that I would die to keep them safe. I think most parents feel that way when they gaze upon their child's face for the first time. An overwhelming wave of love overtakes you, different from any other love that you have experienced before.

It's not just a one-time feeling. It repeats with the birth of each new life and becomes an armor that you wear when you step out with them into the world every day. This sacred feeling is real and tenacious, always on the surface but thankfully seldom tested. Most people never have to lay down their own lives in order to spare the lives of their children.

One of the most profound lessons I took away from my experience, however, is that this instinct is very real. In a life-or-death crisis, it becomes second nature to welcome death in exchange for your child's safety. I begged repeatedly for my rapist to kill me if it meant that my kids would be spared. I would offer my life for them again in a heartbeat, and I am convinced most parents would do the same for their children. Never doubt the strength of this exquisitely pure love.

9

The Fight to Keep Them Alive

BY THE TIME MY abductor began talking about money again, something in me had shifted once more. Fear was still there, but it no longer ruled every thought. I understood that surviving meant more than enduring what he did to my body—it meant staying mentally present, strategic, and alert. If my children were going to live, I would have to think several steps ahead, even while kneeling at his feet.

Before we left the isolation once again, our captor reiterated his need to get the remaining money out of my bank account before he disposed of us. Mustering as much strength and clarity as I could, I once again suggested that if we went to my personal bank, we could most likely get the full amount. I told him that I would do anything, pay any amount of money in the world, to save my kids.

He scoffed at me and said that he had never seen a woman give up so much of her body and dignity to save a child. No mother he ever knew would let herself be used as I did. He went on to say how doubly satisfying it was going to be to watch me lose all of our family's money, along with my virtue. He asked for directions to the bank and hammered out his plan to get access to all of the money as we drove.

Arriving at my bank, a place I often went to in my neighborhood, felt surreal. We were back in an area that I knew like the back of my hand for over twenty-five years. A place that I travelled freely with my kids, with no threat to our safety. I began to grow a little more empowered as I no longer had the weight of geographic uncertainty taking up space in my brain.

Once we exited the Turnpike, my captor pulled the van over to retrieve the clothing that had been flung off my body during the last assault, and I put it on. If I didn't do everything precisely as he instructed, he said that he would flee the bank with my kids in tow while I was inside.

My daughter begged me not to go, not to leave her and her brother alone with the man. I was beyond terrified to be physically separated from my children. I desperately needed to get help if we were going to survive this ordeal, and I knew that he needed them as human collateral to ensure his payoff.

I took a huge deep breath before I opened the van door to go inside. As it cracked open, he yelled, "Stop! I've changed my mind." A new realization came over him, and he screamed, "You can't go into the bank looking like trash. Somebody may recognize you inside and wonder why you have been crying and why your face is all marked up. I'll have to find another way."

It only took a moment for his desperation to morph into a new sinister plan. He decided to move the van parallel to the wall-mounted ATM on the outside edge of the parking lot. There were two drive-thru teller lanes on the other side of the tiny outparcel building. Employees were inside the small building helping drive up clients, but there were no direct eyes on the western outside wall with the ATM, and no security guard outside of the bank that afternoon.

After he screamed at me to get out of the vehicle, I could hear my heart beating in my ears as I stepped away from the van and moved toward the ATM. My daughter cried out as the door shut behind me. I walked carefully up to the ATM and inserted my card. I made direct eye contact with the camera mounted on the ATM in the hopes that it was being monitored somewhere on the premises.

I assumed that because there were workers inside the drive-thru teller building, they might be watching the video on the ATM in case anyone had a problem or was attempting to rob the machine. I could tell that the van was within the sight of the security camera, and this gave me hope. Even if someone didn't respond immediately, maybe in time they would get footage of the driver.

I stood at the ATM for what felt like forever. I first put in my information and legitimately tried to withdraw money from each of our accounts. The screen promptly alerted me after each attempt, though, that I had reached our daily limit and could not take any more money out. I knew my rapist would be furious.

I started to panic about the violence that was in store for my children and me because of not being able to retrieve the funds. This is when I finally decided to signal for help. Looking directly into the camera at the ATM, I slowly and repetitively mouthed "Help Me." While I did this, I also jammed up the buttons so that maybe someone inside the tiny building would pay attention and come to help.

I stayed at the ATM as long as I could, torn between wanting to be reunited with my kids in the van and trying to break free. I could feel his eyes boring holes in the back of my head and, upon glancing back at him, sensed his impatience. I mouthed for help one more time and then returned to the front seat of the van, again strangely confident that help would come soon, now that I was back in my neighborhood.

When I climbed inside the van, I was greeted by the first smile I had seen in hours from my little girl. She was instinctively happy to know I came back to her, and I was thrilled that she could still find a smile somewhere in her heart after the evil of the day. I immediately squeezed my infant son's hand tightly, verbally reassuring them both that I would never leave them again.

Seeing that I had no cash in hand, our abductor sarcastically replied that, actually, I would be leaving them again soon, but this time it would be for the afterlife. Smiles gone. Hope once again shattered. But we were still breathing, so there was still a chance. We would record victories now by surviving from minute to minute.

As he drove out of the parking lot, I was ordered back onto my knees. Just like it all started that day, he commanded me to satisfy him orally while he thought about his next moves out loud. He was desperate for the money still left in the bank accounts, but stumped by how he would get it. He toyed with the idea of coming back for me, maybe the next day and the day after that. We could keep "the party" going until the money was slowly drained out.

"Who would tell on him?" he asked me. Not my kids, he reasoned; my son was an infant, and my daughter was too little to have anyone take her seriously. Not me, he bragged, I was enjoying the thrill of it all too much. According to him, after years of being a pent-up Christian housewife, I finally got to experience the raunchy, uninhibited sex that he knew I wanted. I would be craving him forever now.

He told me that I would just have to come up with a lie for my husband about the bruises, scratches, and swollen eyes, and invent a story about where the money went and what I had been doing all day. As he daydreamed about our future, my cell phone rang, and everything changed again.

10

When Help Was Closest

UP TO THIS POINT, survival had meant fighting against distance as we were driven farther and farther away from anything familiar, anything safe. What came next, though, was more disorienting than isolation. We were brought closer. Closer to home. Closer to people who loved us. Closer to places that had once promised protection. And in that closeness, the danger sharpened.

Hope did not arrive gently. It arrived like a weapon, threatening to break me open if I reached for it. I still held out hope that my cell phone was back at the house in the diaper bag. Strangely, it had not rung all day. I surmised throughout the abduction that it was either dead or just not in the van. I was wrong.

The loud, piercing ring of the cell phone caught everyone off guard, especially my rapist. He must have grown convinced that no one could breach the inside of his sick, twisted bubble, and when they did, he panicked.

He pulled the car over, near the Publix grocery store my family had shopped at for decades, and searched for the phone. Somehow, it had slid along the floor to the back of the van. He looked at the screen and noticed it was my mother calling. This was an event he was not prepared to deal with. There was so much rage in his voice, and we dared not make a sound.

In order to keep me distracted, he ordered me to resume performing oral sex on him. To subdue me, he hit the back of my head with both the butt of the knife and his fist again. He talked softly to himself and then would erratically run his plans by me. At this juncture, he informed me he did not see any more value in keeping us alive. It felt like a bullet to my heart. He said that people would be looking for us, and he did not want to take any risks of getting caught.

He did, however, also romanticize our time together and said that he needed to have my body one more time before he made a final decision. In a strange utterance, he said he wanted me to know that of all the women he had raped over the decades, he loved me the most, and it was the greatest sexual experience he had ever had. The children watching it all were the "icing on the cake" for him. Although my blood curdled when he said it, I felt like if I could exploit this emotion, real or fake, maybe he wouldn't be able to kill us after all.

After driving around for a few minutes, he settled on a location for our final encounter. He chose the park I had grown up playing at, the one adjacent to my elementary school. This was the same park my dad told me about while we were still living in Chicago, a place full of sunshine where we could make happy memories. In fact, the location was directly across the street from my parents' home. In a city of millions of people and places, this stranger unknowingly chose sacred childhood ground.

It was gut-wrenching to see my mom's car in the driveway as we drove past their street. Help had been close many times that day. At the church, in my neighborhood, on the Turnpike, and at the banks, I held out hope that a friend or good Samaritan would save us. Now, the help closest to me was my own mom. I thought about how hard my mom would fight for us if she could, and I like to think that that imagery gave me a boost of special energy and the endurance to survive one more assault.

This final rape on the floor of my van was the most physically brutal assault of the day. He knew he was running out of time. While initially wanting to have a "romantic" last encounter, he was now too overcome with the hatred that had driven him to commit the acts in the first place. He returned to the narrative that he hated women like me and hated their children. All three of us had to be completely destroyed in order to make up for his hellish existence.

He reminded me that no one would ever catch him, and that no God would ever save us. He asked me if I remembered what to do with the evidence when it was time, and I said yes. I continued to keep my eyes closed as he slapped me hard across the face and moved me into position.

His stated plan was to break my body during the last assault. He pushed me physically as far as I was able to go. He said he hadn't shown me what true pain was yet; he had wanted to keep it "civilized." Not anymore. Everything hurt more this time. I think my skin was just too raw, and I was hypersensitive all over. Nothing had grown easier to accept over time, mentally or physically, nor had I become desensitized to the pain.

This attack began like all of the others. He taunted my children again and again about how much God hated them and would never love them as He did before. He told them again that I was a dirty whore and that having him as their dad now was the only thing that might save them. I was growing weaker as the afternoon dragged on, my voice softer. My kids, I am certain, felt even worse than I did, but their cries stayed strong throughout the ordeal. My prayers grew more fervent in my weakness, and I pleaded with God again to send someone to save us.

When my rapist was done with me, he threw my underwear at my face and ordered me to wipe down every single surface of the van to erase his fingerprints. I did as I was told, but tried my best to copy what I had seen heroes on TV crime dramas do. I tried to skip some of the radio and air-conditioning buttons so that I would not destroy everything, but he was wise to my tactics.

Screaming, with the knife back on my neck, I returned to my obedient self and cleaned the entire van to his liking. When I was done, he lay me face down, naked on my stomach, in between my children's two car seats. I felt the car shift into drive, and we were off again. But where to now?

As he drove around the streets I used to play on as a child, he verbalized what he thought the next steps should be. If we survived, I was to drive straight to my house, feed the kids, and put them down for naps. Then, I was supposed to take a hot shower and scrub him off my body, making myself presentable for when I eventually saw my mom and husband later. I should pull myself together and make it seem like nothing unusual happened that day.

He would be watching to make sure I complied, hiding in the nature preserve across the street and peering through the bedroom windows. If I called the police or failed to go straight home, he would be back to kill us immediately. He told me he had a police scanner in his car and would know instantly if I called for help. He threatened that he could get to us before the police did and that we would be stupid to take any chances. I assured him that I understood the instructions and would do exactly as he said.

After our conversation, I felt like there was a real chance that he might let us go. Then, his mind abruptly flipped another switch, and he changed course. He kept repeating the idea that he should probably kill us instead, as it seemed like the safest way to end our time together without him getting caught. He hadn't killed his other victims, but said that things were different this time.

My daughter, he rationalized, might actually be old enough and verbal enough to describe him to the police. He had misjudged her age when he took us, thinking she was younger. In addition, he wasn't sure that I had kept my eyes tightly closed throughout the entire assault. Maybe I was going to be able to identify him after all, especially since we had been so close and intimate multiple times that day. As he drove, my fear grew. It seemed like we were coming to the end of the line, and he was still undecided about how he was going to finish things.

11

When God Did Not Let Go

IT WAS ONLY A few minutes from when we left the park across the street from my parents' house until he stopped the van along overgrown foliage a few miles away. I peeked and realized that we were back at our church. He mumbled about needing to wait until some man in the circular driveway in front of the sanctuary left the area. Then, he spotted a woman walking around the church campus and got frustrated. He needed to park the van somewhere where no one would see us, so he drove through the large parking lots on both sides of the property until he found a suitable place. As soon as he felt we were in the clear, he turned off the ignition.

The air in the van was heavy and stagnant again. My heart started to beat faster than it ever had, my body sensing that everything was almost over. He left the driver's seat for a few moments and used his knife to play with my hair.

He asked my daughter if she thought he should kill me. She let her answer be known through primal screams of "NO!" I reached up and held my son's hand again to soothe him. He had passed out for a couple of minutes but was now growing agitated again. I think my son, even at eight months old, could sense my desperation. The man pressed the knife into the base of my neck, and I rapidly started to process what all this meant.

I remember thinking that this was how I was going to die, naked on the floor of my van with my children on either side of me. I tried to bargain with God, as I assume many people do in their final moments. I begged Him to first save my kids' lives and then my life too, if possible. I promised my eternal faithfulness to Him and vowed to walk through every door He opened for me for the rest of my life if we survived.

Rationally, I knew my God wasn't one to make deals. No amount of pleading or promising was going to change the outcome. I also knew in my heart that His love is unfailing, in both the good times and the bad. The next few minutes would play out with Him in control, no matter what that meant for my family.

What I experienced next was something that I will never, ever forget. It was an irrational feeling of total calm in the middle of extreme chaos. I felt myself letting go in acceptance and slipping away. Why wasn't I gripped with fear about leaving my crying kids behind if I died, alone with the person who had killed their mother? Where was my fight? I had battled all day to save my family, finding strength that I had no idea I even possessed. Now, it felt more natural to succumb to the indescribable peace that enveloped me.

I realize now that in that moment, I knew beyond a shadow of a doubt that God was there holding me close in my greatest time of need. The truth is, I felt Him beside me all day. Throughout the ordeal, my children and I were told that God had abandoned us. Our abductor repeatedly implied that our God would never save us, that He wasn't that powerful.

He taunted that God could never be found amidst all of the profane activities going on inside our van. He yelled that it would be me, in particular, who would die alone and separated from God's love. But that was not true. As our abductor pushed the knife harder against my neck, I felt the terrifying weight of the epic battle lift off my shoulders. I passed out. It was over.

I am not sure how long I was out, but it was probably no more than a minute. I was brought back to life by the piercing screams of my daughter shrieking, "He's gone, Mommy. He's gone. Get up! Get up!" I struggled to muster the little bit of energy I had left inside of me to lift my head, and then my body, off the floor of the van. I pulled myself onto my knees and looked outside the passenger-side windows. The van was surrounded by a huge clump of foliage on the outer edge of the church property. It was an area full of tall Dade County Pines and native brush, making it easy to obscure a vehicle if positioned right. Definitely a secluded spot to start his getaway.

When I shifted my gaze to look directly out of the windshield, I saw him. The man who had frightened me to my core, stripped me of my dignity, and threatened to kill my entire family was boldly walking out in the sunshine, seemingly unafraid of being noticed. He was not trying to fade into his surroundings anymore.

Observing him from afar, I could now get a better approximation of his shape and size. He was still wearing the navy blue T-shirt and drawstring shorts he had on in the van, but appeared a little bit taller and stockier in the full upright position. He didn't have a lot of hair on his head, but what he did have appeared to be medium brown with a reddish tinge. This made sense because I noticed during the assaults that he seemed to have shaved his leg and pubic hair, but what was growing back was a sure mixture of brown and red hues.

What stood out the most to me, though, as I watched him from a distance, was that he had a stark white stripe at the base of his neck that became exposed after a recent buzz-cut from a barber. It was hard for me to believe that this psychopath had a barber, or anyone in his life at all, with whom he engaged civilly.

As he sauntered off down beautiful Old Cutler Road, my favorite street in all of Miami, I realized that he must have been going to retrieve whatever vehicle he had been driving and presumably stashed in a nearby parking lot. This man, all of a sudden, began to seem frightfully human. He was not simply a demonic presence that barged into my life and destroyed it. He was also a person. He was eventually going home. But where could I go? Nowhere in the city felt safe anymore.

While my daughter urgently cried that we needed to look for Daddy, I put on what few pieces of clothing I could gather and gingerly crawled into the driver's seat. My abductor left the keys in the center console, so I snatched them and set out for my husband's office.

We obviously couldn't go home. The man said he would be there. However, within about twenty seconds of driving, I realized that it was a terrible plan. I was only partially dressed, and Jamie's office was at least thirty minutes away. I had no idea where my phone was, and I didn't want to waste time looking. I needed to get us to safety as fast as I could.

Then I remembered that my mother was home. I assured Mia that we would be at Grandma and Grandpa's house very soon, and that seemed to calm her down. My parents' house was one of her happy places. Her sobs faded into whimpers as we sped away from the church. When we arrived at my childhood home, the place I had sought comfort in after all of life's previous traumas, I jumped out of the van and locked it behind me.

I opened the garage door and ran screaming like a maniac into the kitchen. As luck would have it, my mother was on the phone with my father. They were going out of town the next day and were finishing up travel plans. My mom took one look at me and shrieked in horror, "Oh my God, Julie!" She dropped the phone immediately and ran to hug me. I pushed her away like she was a predator too and wildly screamed, "Don't touch me … don't ever touch me! I have been raped. Help the kids."

I will always remember the look of sheer terror in my mom's eyes as I witnessed her heart literally breaking into pieces before my eyes. I tossed her the keys to the van, and she flew out the garage door like a bat out of hell to find the children in the van. Sobbing, I picked the phone up and started to tell my father what happened. I was thirty-one years old, and I had never heard my father's voice so intense, like he was about to jump through the phone and shake me.

"Hang up and call the police … call 9-1-1 right now!" I wept into the phone, "I can't, Dad, he promised that he will kill us," defying my father's orders for one of the few times in my life. I was hysterical, honestly believing that if I broke my promise to the rapist, I was signing my family's death warrant.

Our abductor had been so clear about what the plan was to be if I survived the attacks. I had already broken my promise to him that I would go straight home, take a shower, and feed the kids. Under no circumstances was I to call the police. He threatened to kill us from the first moment he ambushed us in the church parking lot and informed me throughout the day that he had a police scanner in his car and would know if I ever reached out for help.

He knew where we lived and where we went to church. At my core, I was too terrified to pick up the phone and make the most obvious call of my life. Over the years, more people than I can believe have told me that I was "lucky" to be raped by a stranger; I think they speculated that being assaulted by an unknown attacker must have made calling the police a no-brainer. While I understand why people might make that assumption, picking up the phone and calling 9-1-1 in that moment was one of the hardest and riskiest things I have ever done. As I dialed those three numbers, I felt like I was going to die all over again.

12

When Silence Broke

THE POLICE DISPATCHER WHO picked up the call calmly and matter-of-factly asked me what my emergency was. Choking on my own tears, I told her that I had just been carjacked and raped at knifepoint by an unknown assailant in my van. You could hear the urgency in her voice grow as she asked me if I knew where he was and if she could have the address that I was calling from. I told her that I didn't know his present location and that I was scared to give her the address where I was because he said he would kill my two kids and me.

She grew very firm with me and told me that I had to tell her where I was; she raised her voice in audible concern and said I had to report the rape. The dispatcher's tone mirrored my father's insistence. When she put the pieces together and realized that it was not just me in the van, she asked with trepidation, "Did he rape you in front of the kids?" I started sobbing, "Yes," and she replied in horror, "Oh my God...."

After we hung up, I called my husband's office to see if he was safe. I was terrified he wouldn't be there. Had our perpetrator, in fact, harmed him too? When his coworker answered the call and heard me crying, he quickly ran to find Jamie. Thank God he was unharmed, and that it had all been a lie the man had cooked up to intensify our fear and further force our compliance.

Over the course of a marriage, there are many difficult conversations that spouses have—this would be our toughest by far. I knew that as soon as I opened my mouth and told him what happened, I would break his heart at the most fundamental level. Jamie's life would now be changed forever too. I didn't want to do that to him.

The words took on a special sense of urgency, however, as soon as I heard his familiar, concerned voice. After audibly gasping in shock over the news, he gathered all of his strength and said he was on his way home. Both my husband and my father miraculously made it home from work that day in record time.

Within about three minutes of my original 9-1-1 call, a Miami-Dade County police car arrived at my parents' house. A female officer, whose kindness I will never forget, entered the house through the open garage door and was led into the kitchen by my frightened mom. When our eyes met, and I saw the officer's badge and her gun, I knew that I was finally safe.

That feeling had eluded me all day, every step of the way. Help always seemed close, but distinctly out of reach. The look in the officer's eyes and her initial demeanor conveyed an unspoken message of compassion and professionalism. I could finally exhale now. It felt amazing to breathe in hope again.

The responding officer ushered me back into my childhood bedroom, where I curled up in the fetal position on my old bed. The four walls were no stranger to my joys or my heartbreaks over the decades. I am so grateful I still had that space to comfort me during the worst day of my adult life. I closed my eyes and cried into a pillow, releasing a strange mix of feelings—gratitude for being alive, searing pain from the injuries, and, most of all, intense worry for the mental and physical health of my kids, whom I still had not seen.

After finding them in the van in those first few moments after the assaults, my mom immediately took them across the street to a trusted neighbor's house to keep them out of the chaos while law enforcement did their work. Although I was extremely grateful that they were safe and being wrapped in love and kindness, I was extremely panicked to be apart from them. My heart burned with primal desperation to be with my babies.

Adding to my physical discomfort at the time was my urgent need to use the bathroom and have a glass of water. I needed those two basic things right away. With sadness in her eyes, the responding officer told me I could not do either. I could see on her face that she felt horrible having to deny my requests. The officer explained that my body was now considered a crime scene and had to be preserved as such.

A crime scene? Unfortunately, she was right. It's hard to explain, but immediately after we escaped the nightmare, I felt like an alien on earth. My view of my physical being was starting to morph now too. I felt like a petri dish. An object to be studied. My skin no longer felt like it fit correctly over my bones; all of the softness had disappeared. I felt dirty to my core. The pit in my stomach seemed bottomless. It felt as if he had stolen my very soul.

Jamie's arrival at my parents' house jolted me back to the tasks at hand. When he showed up, he was immediately directed by officers to go across the street to be with our children and my mom. I know that for him, seeing that his precious children were still alive, made October 16 the most profound day of his life, next to their births.

My own dad arrived at the house just moments after Jamie did and raced down the hall to find me with the officer in my old room. I am sure he felt just like Jamie did, overcome with joy to see his child alive. My dad quickly sat down on my old desk chair and listened to every word I told the officer about my ordeal.

It was extremely painful to recount what had happened in front of him. It was difficult to see tears in my father's eyes. The questions were embarrassingly invasive, but, thankfully, the first responder who was asking them leaned into both her humanity and training. We struggled through the painful narrative the best we could.

As we spoke in the immediate aftermath of my rapes, I felt confident that my responding officer wanted to catch the perpetrator as much as I did. She seemed invested in the case already and calmly walked me through the steps of what was going to happen next. She emphasized how important it was for me to trust her.

She took copious notes about my experience and, in return, shared vital procedural information with me. She explained that a specialized detective from the Sex Crimes Division was on the way and that they would ensure I received the proper medical care. I cannot stress enough how comforting it was to feel that I was not alone in what was happening.

I didn't fully appreciate the gift of her competence and assurances until after the fact, but she definitely set a positive tone at the onset of my interactions with law enforcement. I would sadly come to learn years later that not every victim finds themselves as lucky as I was that day.

The responding officer and I had only been together for a short time when a sex crimes detective entered the sanctum of my childhood bedroom. I was quickly introduced to Detective KL, and with that, the two law enforcement officers present traded off responsibilities. I was sad to see the initial officer step aside since I felt so comfortable with her. She was the person I felt had "saved" me after the 9-1-1 call and was the first person I told the details of my story to.

I got nervous that the next officer, a male detective, might not be as sensitive or understand my motherly fears as well as the female officer had. Fortunately, Detective KL turned out to be every bit as professional as the responding officer had been. He had specialized training in the unique needs that sexual assault victims have and clearly understood the protocols of how these types of investigations should proceed.

He exuded an aura of strength and knowledge that was much appreciated by both me and my father, who was still close by to advocate for me and ask questions when it became clear that I wasn't clearly processing some of the information. The detective's approach was no-nonsense but very much rooted in compassion.

It was hard to start the story about what happened to me over again so quickly. I felt vulnerable and embarrassed by many of the things that had happened to me, and telling them to someone new, especially to a man, made me feel viscerally ill. Detective KL asked for more comprehensive details than I had shared with the responding officer, and as I described the brutality of it all, my heart pumped wildly. I truly started to feel like the assaults were happening all over again. This time, however, my mind began to truly process the words I was saying, and I became uniquely horrified by them.

I almost couldn't believe what had just happened to my children and me, although I had just lived it. Would the people I told about the event be able to believe it too? The detective let me talk as long as I wanted to and share everything I was comfortable telling him at the time. He took notes and responded to questions. I felt believed, but as an individual who was completely unfamiliar with crime or law enforcement procedures, I was still profoundly lost.

Towards the end of the talk, Detective KL explained that I would need to be transported to a rape crisis center (RCC), where I would be treated for my injuries, and evidence would be collected. The RCC in Miami-Dade County was located in the heart of downtown, at Jackson Memorial Hospital (JMH). I was no stranger to the name. This was the same hospital that housed the county's trauma center, which I had been airlifted to after my car accident in my senior year of high school.

Back then, I flatlined several times in the emergency room there and almost lost my life. I lived in that hospital for close to a month while I was in a coma, received blood transfusions, and underwent several surgeries to save my left arm. I left that hospital in a wheelchair, unable to walk due to a shattered pelvis. Suffice it to say, it was not a place that I ever wanted to return to. It was the only other place on earth, besides the Everglades now, that I associated with dying. My body stiffened at the thought of going there.

My father saw the fear in my eyes when the detective talked about the hospital, and before I could scream "No!" he intervened. He explained my reaction to the detective and demanded that I be taken to a much closer hospital for treatment since there were three of them within about 10 miles of my parents' home. My dad wanted me to be seen as quickly as possible and not be retraumatized by going back to JMH.

I naturally agreed with him. I just wanted this part to be over so I could reunite with my husband and kids. It would be at least an hour to get to the rape crisis center downtown, maybe even longer with traffic. The southern suburbs of the county had exploded in population since my family moved to the area in 1978, and the roads into the city of Miami were jammed at all hours. This logistical fact, coupled with the PTSD from my accident, made me cry and beg to go anywhere else, as if my life depended on it.

Detective KL stood his ground and persuasively explained why we needed to trust him and go to the RCC. It was the county's official protocol for sexual assault victims. I had no idea what this meant, but I listened closely as he walked us through the reasoning.

First, he addressed the logistical issues that we were concerned about, mainly the length of time it would take to get to the hospital. He explained that, unlike in a traditional ER, I would not be triaged behind other cases and would be seen immediately. There were no insurance forms or stacks of paperwork to be filled out by the patient, like there were in standard emergency rooms. He also said that I would not have to wait my turn to be seen by sitting in a mass waiting room, where other patients would wonder why I was escorted by a police officer. It would ultimately be the faster and more private option.

More importantly, the detective explained that I would see a specially trained forensic nurse, also known as a sexual assault nurse examiner (SANE). This nurse would take me into a private room close to the ER so that I could openly explain the physical details of my assault and have a rape kit done. I did not know what to expect during the exam itself and was scared. I had heard about a rape kit and how important the contents were in solving violent crimes, but had never actually seen this part of a rape victim's experience played out in TV dramas or books.

The detective assured me that a professional SANE could competently tend to my medical needs while also expertly collecting evidence from various places on my body. The nurse would do both of those things with extensive training in victim-centered care.

I am forever grateful to Detective KL for taking the time to explain the benefits of my making the trek to JMH, even though initially I was opposed to the idea. The simple sharing of "why" going to the RCC was the better option calmed my nerves and made me feel like I wasn't just being thrown blindly into a random system. I was comforted by knowing that there was a special plan in place to help people like me. Although I felt like a mutant, I was clearly not alone in this experience.

Detective KL ended up staying back at my parents' house to secure my van, preserving whatever evidence was hopefully inside. Thankfully, the responding officer was still on the scene and was able to drive me all the way down to the RCC, officially referred to as the Roxcy Bolton Rape Treatment Center.

Getting into the police car and being driven for over an hour to the center provoked a different kind of anxiety in me. I had some quiet time in the car to think. What filled my mind was not a specific feeling that my life was immediately in danger, but rather the growing weight of the separation from my family members, especially my children.

Although the sweet and seasoned officer assured me during our lengthy drive that my children were being well cared for by family and law enforcement, not being able to speak with them made them feel like they were a million miles away. I made a foolish vow to myself right then and there that they would never leave my sight again. This was not very popular with them once they became teenagers.

13

Preserved

MY STOMACH TWISTED INTO knots as we approached the hospital, and I saw signs for the trauma center and the helipad. I knew driving to the place where I had almost died years before was going to have an unpredictable effect on my psyche. I got distracted from focusing on the rape and became flooded with memories of the accident. Strangely, however, I ended up finding a little bit of strength in those memories. The barrage of images flipping through my brain about the crash and the rehabilitation was proof that I could survive trauma. Maybe I would survive the torture of this visit too.

While my previous time at JMH was one of lifesaving medical urgency, the current visit was distinctly different. This time, I was there to be thoroughly examined and have medical professionals collect the necessary biological evidence needed to capture the dangerous psychopath who tortured my family. Both visits to the hospital were frighteningly serious, and each became a matter of life or death for me. Severe physical injury and psychological fear feel strangely similar.

I was jolted back to my present awareness when the police car stopped outside of an unassuming, unmarked door on the hospital's campus. As the door closed solidly behind the officer and me, I felt a sense of calm. It was a feeling that was vastly different from the frantic intensity of the day. There were no sounds of screaming, no crying, no traffic horns. No sensory overload. It was empty and peaceful, very different from what I expected from a space dedicated to treating patients who had just experienced violent crime.

There was a small space for me to wait in while the detective spoke softly with a woman behind a desk. She said that she had been expecting us. There was a TV on behind her, and it was broadcasting news about the kidnapping and the assaults from outside of my parents' home. It felt surreal to see the story on the news before I had even seen a doctor. The woman at the desk instinctively turned it off when she saw me nervously watching.

After only a few minutes, a nurse came to guide me back to a private examination area. The officer assured me that she would wait at the hospital until I was finished. It made me feel secure to know that she was staying. It sounds like such a small act of kindness, but it felt magnified under the circumstances. I did not want to be left on my own in a system I knew nothing about. Being with the officer and at an RCC felt like I was thrown a life preserver from my community.

Again, I did not know how fortunate I was in those moments that Miami had these established protocols to aid with victim care. Inside the exam space, I met my SANE or forensic nurse. She is another person that I remember from that day with crystal clear detail. I could tell from the onset of our interactions that this was not going to be like any of my previous times in an emergency room. She was kind but notably professional in her approach. She looked me in the eyes when she introduced herself and let me know with a special warmth that she would be in this with me for as long as it took.

She reiterated that she was there to help me and that I could feel safe with her. She was not there to judge me, but rather to help heal me, both through treating my physical body and caring for my emotional concerns. When this initial introduction ended, she asked me to get undressed, put on a gown, and lie back on the exam table.

"Breathe deeply," the nurse instructed. Nothing can prepare a person for what a sexual assault exam is like. The messaging that goes out to the general population from public safety officials, and especially TV media and news networks, rarely ever tries. In part, I think this is because it is a profoundly raw experience that almost defies explanation. It is so acutely personal, and sometimes painful.

What I took away from my time on the examination table is that treatment by a specially trained SANE professional is one of the first important steps in setting the tone for a victim's journey. I say this both in terms of a person's individual healing and their potential participation in the justice system moving forward.

Letting another person see me for the first time, in all of my post-rape nakedness, was terrifying. I felt like a completely different person than I was when I woke up that day. My intimate areas felt like they had been through war, ugly and damaged. My entire body felt like it had no shred of dignity left, and I felt cloaked in shame. I never wanted anyone in the whole world to see me or touch me again. Was there a document I could sign to ensure that?

While daydreaming about my "imaginary no touching ever again agreement," I was suddenly snapped back to reality. I wanted to run away when the nurse asked me to place my feet in the exam table's stirrups and to try to relax. Relax? Was she kidding?

It was almost easier for me to relax when a psychopath pushed a butcher knife against my neck and threatened to kill me than it was when the nurse asked me to lift up my gown. Her steady encouragement, however, sustained me. She told me that she, too, was shaken by what had happened to me, and she wanted to treat and document my injuries as thoroughly as possible.

This would, unfortunately, entail uncomfortable poking and prodding in my violated areas and full exposure at times. In addition to cooperating with her to heal my injured parts, she needed me to give precise details of the rape to know where to best search for evidence. My nurse said I needed to be strong throughout the exam and to trust her completely. She eventually led me to a space psychologically where I could do that. I surrendered my body to her.

This would be my third time in just a few short hours that I had to tell my story over again. The sixth time, if you count my parents, husband, and the 9-1-1 operator hearing the earliest snippets of the assaults. I was exhausted from talking, especially since the interviews were getting longer and more intimate each time. Something about my nurse, however, gave me the strength to dig deep and disclose the most graphic details of the physical abuse. Maybe it was her unhurried approach in listening to me, or maybe because my body was already in her hands, being examined inch by inch, but I felt at ease despite my very undignified state.

I warned her early on that she may not find DNA in areas where she was used to seeing it, due to my assailant's preoccupation with destroying the biological evidence. She took very detailed notes about each assault and swabbed, both internally and externally, every affected body part.

While she combed my entire body for hairs and fluids, conversation grew quiet. During this time, I prayed fervently, and somewhat uncomfortably, that some small speck of him remained on my skin. I knew that I would never rest until he was identified. She went on and collected blood samples and ran a pregnancy test on me to see if I was already pregnant by my husband before the rape. The imminent threat of pregnancy from the rapes was just another fear I suddenly got to add to my list of frightful experiences on this bizarre journey.

While my rapist had taken care not to directly ejaculate into my vagina, memories of high school biology and the nurse's musings reminded me that preejaculatory fluid can still pose a risk. The test quickly came back negative for preassault pregnancy, but a test to see if I was pregnant from the rape wouldn't happen for a few more days. I was offered a dose of emergency contraception to stop the fertilization and implantation of any embryo that resulted from the rape.

I was paralyzed by what to do. Since college, I had been staunchly pro-choice for other women, but not for myself. I felt like, due to my faith, my personal options were very limited. There was some controversy around emergency contraception in religious circles, but since I never thought it would affect me, I never stopped long enough to define my views on it.

After a day of listening to twisted scripture from my rapist, my mind and beliefs felt altogether scrambled. I craved having a close friend or family member with me in the hospital, someone that I could seek spiritual guidance from. I prayed fervently.

Luckily for me that night, my nurse gave me both comfort and good medical information. She did not attempt to sway my decision but made sure I understood exactly what the pill would and would not do. She allowed me to call my father from the exam table, and I cried into the phone, pleading for his advice and support.

He said exactly what I needed to hear at that moment and reminded me to trust my heart. I knew deep down that for me, taking the oral pill was the right choice for my body. It would stop the embryo from implanting from the start and would prevent me from having to make even tougher choices later on. I felt at peace with my decision. In hindsight, I see now how my initial confusion over what to do was actually one of the first blessings that came out of my trauma.

My compassion for others in similar situations grew exponentially at the RCC. I got to experience firsthand, deep in my soul, how excruciatingly difficult choices like that are for women, and how outside judgment has no place inside a patient's exam room. No one knows the choices they may have to make someday, especially when the world hands them an unfortunate situation they never imagined being in.

I made a note to myself that night that the world needed to replace its constant judgment with gentleness. Sometimes people find themselves in dark places that others will never fully understand unless they go there themselves. Trust the ones who have experienced the crisis, who have walked through the fire, to know what is best for their life. It is between them and their Creator alone.

With the pregnancy protocols and some of my philosophical wonderings behind me, it was at this point that my nurse took out a camera to photograph my injuries. That moment reopened a new layer of vulnerability. My humiliation returned in spades at the thought of strangers potentially seeing intimate pictures of my bruised and damaged body in court or anywhere else. It took some coaxing, but the nurse once again explained to me how important this part of the process was and said that if I someday wanted justice for what happened to my family and me, I would need to cooperate and allow her to photograph me.

I lay on the table and followed her directions. She was not kidding when she told me that trust was at the heart of our time together. Our rapport was the only thing pleasant about the situation. She was an angel among all of the chaos. Unfortunately, though, I started to feel like an object being photographed for an auction on eBay, having to turn and twist, exposing every side for others to peruse.

By this point, we were nearing the end of my physical examination and the collection of vital evidence. The first order of business after the exam ended was to quench my thirst and hunger. I had not eaten any food since dinner the previous night, well over twenty-four hours prior. I had only sipped from a cup of water after I brushed my teeth that morning. My body was starving and definitely dehydrated.

It is amazing to note, however, that when a person is in survival mode, these essential components of existence lose their urgency in order to preserve their focus on the fight. Now, these primal needs emerged with a vengeance. I was desperate to be nourished, but mostly looking forward to the moment when I could rid the horrible tastes of the day from my mouth. I could still taste him. That realization made my stomach churn. The nurse sincerely apologized and said that there was no food to be had, although I was given a cup of water to sip and swish around, which made me feel a bit more human.

While I sat there, I was also growing more uncomfortable with my continued exposure in the medical gown. Other people besides the nurse had come in, including the police, and I just wanted to wear actual clothes when I interacted with them. I had only been given a pair of disposable paper underwear to cover me underneath my gown, which were rough and scratchy on my injured genital area.

The nurse explained that my husband was sending me an outfit to wear to the police station, but it could still be an hour before it arrived. I made another note to myself that when all of this was over, future rape victims would have access to soft cotton underwear and a toothbrush immediately. Maybe even some mouthwash. Many years later, I made good on my promise.

After a while, a fresh set of clothes arrived at the RCC, wrapped up like a care package. Everything inside smelled like the comfort and safety of home. Jamie had packed it for me and included my favorite T-shirt, my childhood blanket, and a sweet picture of the family from our recent vacation to Disney.

I relished the smiles on my kids' faces in the photo. It helped erase, for just a moment, the terrified expressions I last saw them wearing. So much of the victim experience during and after a sexual assault is rooted in sensory memories. Putting on the soft clothing felt like being hugged by the sender. Seeing the picture reminded me of what I had waiting for me at home.

This alone gave me the strength to put one foot in front of the other when I was told that there were still other stops I had to make before reaching that beloved destination. I was anxious, but determined, to proceed through the next steps to the best of my ability as I left the security of the exam room.

I thought we were headed to the police car again, but there was one more stop. After leaving the medical area, I was directed to an adjoining space where I was met by an advocate at the RCC. I was given many pamphlets and kindly advised about the resources I could access now that I was part of the Miami-Dade County victim services program.

The advocate explained to me the purpose of the blood samples and swabs they had taken in order to determine my exposure to potential sexually transmitted infections (STIs) from my offender. She dispensed prophylactic medications to me in case I ended up testing positive and said that I would need to come back in about two weeks for the results of my HIV screening.

I started to cry again. It was stressful and humbling to realize that after a lifetime of intentionally avoiding casual sex and disease exposure, I was now 100 percent at risk for whatever STIs my offender was carrying.

I thought back to the earliest part of the assault when I had awkwardly begged him to use a condom. He laughed directly in my face and explained how much he was going to relish the feeling of being deep inside of my body after months of shower sex with men in prison. I started to fear for my life all over again.

It seemed like everywhere I turned, I encountered a new batch of consequences attached to my rape. I needed food and someone to calm me down as debilitating thoughts swirled in my head. The responding officer waited for me to finish my exam just as she promised, and I was subsequently introduced to another female officer, Detective JH. She was going to drive me to the central police station in Miami-Dade, where I would have another interview with the police and meet with a sketch artist. At this point, I was weak and couldn't even remember what day it was. I told her I was afraid that anything I was saying at this point was coming out indecipherable since my blood sugar was so low.

One of my most vivid memories of that time together is how she pulled into an all-night drive-thru and bought me a cheeseburger, fries, and a drink. It was a Miami Subs near the hospital, all lit up in neon Miami Vice colors. I mentally noted that the colorful lights blinking before me stood in deep contrast to the mood of my soul.

As I ate what little I actually could stomach of the meal, I cracked a smile for the first time all night, reflecting on the ridiculous tableau. I felt empowered to make it to the central station and go through the events of the previous day once again. When that was over, it was time to meet the sketch artist.

14

In the Face of Evil

I WAS VERY SCARED by the notion of meeting with a sketch artist. For people who have not been a victim of violent crime, this may sound weird, as it seems like one of the least invasive parts of the process. In my mind, however, this sketch was going to be crucial in catching him. If he had been successful in destroying the DNA and eliminating other identifying evidence— fingerprints, body hair, anything physical at all—this sketch might be the only thing left to ID him with.

I tried hard to steal glimpses of him when I could during our time together, but the bulk of the time, my eyes remained tightly closed to avoid eye contact. I could not fathom being able to recreate his face with the disconnected details I remembered. What terrified me most was the possibility that no tangible evidence had remained behind. The pressure I felt was indescribable. I needed this person caught ASAP to ensure the safety of my family and community. If nothing remained—no evidence, no likeness, no proof—there would be no peace. Without him behind bars, I could never feel safe again.

Fortunately, our case that night landed on the desk of a young woman whose skill was already becoming legendary in South Florida. In 1999, Samantha Steinberg's talent and passion were absolutely undeniable, and she became the very first person to hold the title of

Forensic Artist in Miami-Dade County. In 2001, she was chosen by the FBI to attend their Forensic Facial Imaging course.

In the early morning hours of October 17, 2002, just one year after her FBI training was completed, she sat across a desk from me, calmly encouraging my mind to search for whatever details might still remain. At first, it felt hopeless. However, her easy demeanor allowed my mind to relax enough to allow imprints of his face to solidify in my mind. What had once felt fragmented slowly took shape. Then she handed me a huge binder full of random faces, hundreds and hundreds of faces. When I saw a feature that resembled his, a nose or a pair of eyes, I would stop and tell her.

It took hours, but in the end, she compiled a composite sketch that I felt closely resembled my attacker. It was unsettling how much of him had survived my fear and his threats. Maybe others wouldn't be able to recognize him from the sketch, but in my mind, I felt that it was very accurate—and horrifying.

After surviving a day filled with terror and completing countless visits with agencies around the City of Miami, it was finally time for Detective JH to drive me home. Unfortunately, "home" was not to be my actual house, where I lived with my husband and kids, but rather my parents' house. The police suggested that I should stay there indefinitely, just in case the perpetrator came back to find me.

My parents had waited up through the night for my return and hugged me close when I opened the door. Receiving physical touch, of any kind, felt miserable and uncomfortable. I did not want it, and yet, I needed it just as much as they did. There were lots of tears flowing as I collapsed into them. After a tall glass of water and a tranquilizer, the next step was the shower.

I know that this sounds redundant, but I cannot overstate how surreal it felt to be back in that childhood space. In my old home, standing in the bathroom where I got ready for school every day growing up, where I had collapsed unconscious the night before my high school graduation, where I got ready for my wedding, and where my water had broken before Mia's birth. There was a bittersweet comfort in it all.

Standing there alone in the bathroom, I gingerly removed my clothes and turned on the water. I loved hot showers, but this one would be scalding—and an unpleasant one, too, as I quickly realized being naked was an excruciating sensation. With intention and strength, I stepped into the tub, grabbed a washcloth and soap, and began to scrub my body.

I scrubbed hard for what felt like an eternity, trying to remove the essence of my rapist from my skin. I attacked my own flesh with vigor to remove the stench of the day, the feeling of his hands all over me, and the sense that I would feel dirty forever. When I was done, I stood underneath the stream of water like a limp rag doll and cried softly until there were no tears left.

I slept that first night home fairly soundly, thanks to the tranquilizers and the absolute physical exhaustion I was experiencing. When I finally woke up the next afternoon to the sun streaming into my old bedroom and a hush throughout the house, it almost felt like it had all just been a bad nightmare. As I started to move, however, I noticed that all of my muscles felt sore, and I had bruises darkening rapidly all over my body.

A look in the mirror confirmed that what I was experiencing was definitely not a dream. Reality set in, and everything that had happened came creeping back to me in technicolor. I felt panicked and needed to see Jamie and the kids at once.

The night before, when Jamie called his family with the news of the abduction and assaults, my sweet mother- and father-in-law immediately bought tickets to fly from Pennsylvania to Miami to be with us. My brother-in-law and sister-in-law, who were living in London at the time, did the same. They would all land that night, so Jamie brought the kids to my parents' house to see me before company arrived.

Finally being reunited with my husband and kids that afternoon at my parents' house was almost indescribable. My words will never do the experience justice. Feeling their warm hugs and gazing on their sweet faces was like experiencing the most intense and pure love in all the world. It felt similar to the emotion I experienced after each of their births, holding them for the first time.

We had just been to hell and experienced evil on earth, but we were very much alive and together again. Nothing in the world mattered more to me than the people standing right in front of me. I teared up, feeling once again like I had been given the most sacred gift in life: a family. I struggled to hold my emotions together for the sake of the children's peace, and Jamie's too.

I am so blessed that, in my absence, they had such a wonderful and devoted father who would protect them and love them from the depths of his soul. With him and the rest of our family taking care of the kids, I knew that I could focus on what I had to do now, which was to focus on my health.

In those first seventy-two hours after the crime, I rested, saw a psychologist, called my closest friends, and was medically examined by some of my old doctors who had treated me after my car accident over a decade before. Due to the head injury that I received when I was originally struck on my skull and from the repeated punches I sustained to the back of my head during the assaults in the van, I was back in contact with my old neurologist.

The repeated strikes to my reconstructed left elbow had left significant bruising and required me to see my beloved orthopedic surgeon for the first time since a surgery with her years before. The reunions were wonderful, yet totally bizarre, filled with tears and hugs instead of smiles. We were all left dumbfounded by the circumstances. It was like worlds were being brought together again by my successive tragedies. As different as the former and current instances were, repeat appearances by some of the same doctors proved to be remarkably comforting in my immediate healing.

While my parents and I dealt with my immediate physical issues and mental health, Jamie and his family were extremely busy at their end, trying to create an environment of safety and calm in our home. The house was filled with family, which was a great distraction for the kids and helped them feel more secure. Nana and Pop Pop loved to cook and read stories to them, so the inside of the home took on a cozy feel despite the police and occasional media presence outside.

During this time, plans were being hatched by some of the playgroup girls at church to have Peter baptized in the upcoming week or two, while my out-of-town family was still in Florida. Mia had been baptized surrounded by family at our church as an infant two years prior, wearing the traditional Weil family christening gown. I wanted the same for Peter, but had been delayed in making plans.

The unfortunate events of October 16 provided a catalyst to finally set up the baptismal event, which had now taken on even more importance for Jamie and me. Peter could have been murdered in the van just days prior, and we felt overcome with extreme joy and reverence now every time we held him in our arms. Unfortunately, looking into his sweet face reminded me of how my rapist said I would never again be able to do so without remembering the assault. I was determined to take away that power. We wanted to stand in front of the congregation, just as we had done with Mia years before, and dedicate Peter's life to God, thanking Him and promising to raise him up in the faith.

The baptism/dedication would happen about ten days after the attack, during the main Sunday service. Jamie took care of the plans, enlisting my dearest playgroup friends to help with the ceremony details. I was graciously left to simply absorb the information about place and time and work on building up my courage to return to our church.

I was scared to go back. Simple trips to favorite places were now events that would require unusual amounts of courage. Joyfully, every pew was filled, and chairs spilled out into the vestibule as community members and church members packed the building and enveloped us with love. It was a very powerful experience to have so many neighbors hold us up as we made this special covenant with God. The police were there, too, of course, in case our abductor came back and tried to mix in with the crowd.

15

The Evidence That Remained

IT IS IMPORTANT TO mention that just a few days after the attack, Jamie was instructed by the police to take our daughter Mia to the Kristi House in downtown Miami, adjacent to Jackson Memorial Hospital. I had heard bits and pieces about this place over the years and knew that the organization's purpose was to help children who had experienced sexual abuse and other childhood trauma. For years, I wanted to get more involved with the organization, but I hadn't found time yet as a young mom.

I assumed that season of service would come later, after my children were older, after life slowed down. Instead, almost overnight, I became deeply involved with Kristi House because we desperately needed their services. They were now among the first professionals who would directly interact with my children about the event, outside of family and neighbors.

These individuals would help set the tone for my children's healing, especially my daughter's. I prayed for their wisdom and their kindness as they held my daughter's loving, innocent heart in their hands. I didn't want her to be exposed to anything else that would scare her, but we had no choice but to trust the system—one that had not failed us yet.

Mia was summoned to Kristi House primarily to participate in her forensic interview for the police. I wanted to go with her since

I knew how delicate the visit would be, but I was told to stay home. My previous knowledge of the organization's stellar reputation and assurances from law enforcement that she was in the best of hands made it easier for me to let her go with Jamie that day.

At the facility, the questioning was both extensive and brutal for a girl so small and young, but Jamie and the other professionals involved assured me that she did great. She engaged in play therapy and interacted with a skilled child forensic interviewer. The conversations were recorded in a safe, kid-friendly environment.

My daughter shared what information she could about what she saw and what the man had said to her while we were with him. She also gave basic details about what he looked like. My daughter was a true rock star that day and remained one throughout the process. My son, too, although he experienced the trauma of the day in a different way. I am grateful to have had skilled forensic psychologists involved in my daughter's testimony from the start.

The following days were filled with a whirlwind of activity. I felt numb inside, like I was completely disconnected from my body and mind at this point in order to preserve my sanity. The police sent a team of officers over to my parents' house several times, first to transcribe an official statement from me and then to photograph my injuries and developing bruises.

Patrol cars were stationed outside of both my parents' house and my own residence as well for security purposes. The media was omnipresent, too, as the story was at the top of the local news cycle for weeks that fall. I grew accustomed to phone calls and visits from Detectives KL and JH, as well as a new female detective, Detective MV.

Within the first couple of days of the investigation, I was informed by law enforcement that no biological evidence from my perpetrator was found in my rape kit, despite my being raped four times. By the end of the first week, I was also told that the crime scene investigators recovered no physical evidence from my van.

My rapist had been with me for what felt like a lifetime. How did he escape without leaving a single hair or fingerprint? It seemed inconceivable. It was all playing out exactly like he said it would; he would never be identified and never be caught. These words were now amplified in my head. The tiny speck of hope I held onto that he would be apprehended started growing fainter and fainter. I was terrified of what a future with him on the run meant for my family's lives. I cried very hard that night. Unfortunately for him, however, I prayed even harder.

Miraculously, after receiving the demoralizing news that there was no forensic evidence found in my case, my spirits were unexpectedly lifted just a few days later. While I was sitting around my parents' dinner table with my in-laws and the kids, all of us trying our best to make light conversation, the phone rang. It was the police calling for me.

I slinked away to take the call in a back room for privacy. On the line was one of my detectives with astonishing news. They had a solid lead. It turns out the forensic analyst, in my case, had tested more than just the biological swabs from my rape kit at the lab. My clothes became the first key to his downfall.

As it turns out, this particular analyst responsible for testing took it upon herself to actually complete two additional levels of testing on the items collected by the police at the hospital. She tested my foundation garments and my clothes.

Sometimes, when the initial rape kit yields no evidence, the process stops. Body swabs from the victim are the most likely source of usable DNA in a rape case, and when they are negative, other testing is not always pursued. Occasionally, however, a victim's bra and underwear will be tested for evidence since they are the next most likely items to be exposed to fluids during a sexual assault. In my case, that level of testing was not going to yield anything since my undergarments had been taken off me early on and never worn again.

As expected, the analyst's testing on these items came up negative. Thankfully, she was as thorough as possible and continued on with testing my outer garments as well. It was definitely a long shot that anything at all would be found. But this is where my case took an incredible turn, and my analyst became my angel.

Shockingly, she recovered a tiny spot of mixed DNA from the front of the Tinkerbell shirt I was wearing that day. It was a very small sample, most likely the combination of my saliva and a few specks of ejaculate. It must have transferred from my lips onto the collar of the shirt after the first rape, when he gave it back to me to put on so that I could interact with the drive-up teller. I truly don't know where I would be today without that miracle DNA recovery.

The first part of the miracle is that the shirt was tested at all. There was no visible staining on it, and it wasn't part of the police report. I told officers that I was naked for almost 100 percent of the time that we were missing. If the first two levels of testing yielded nothing, there was presumably little value in looking at the top or shorts.

The second part of the DNA miracle was that the Miami-Dade Crime Lab had the capability, through advanced technology, to test a mixed sample like that. Testing DNA mixtures in 2002 was a very complex undertaking in the world of forensic science, and few labs had the equipment to do it accurately at that time. It sounds crazy to say, but I count myself lucky every day that I was raped in Miami, where they had recently invested in cutting-edge DNA technology. If I had been raped in most other parts of the US, I may not have had the same outcome.

The first big break in the case came when the sample from my shirt was analyzed and uploaded into the FBI's CODIS database. It matched another male DNA profile from the same area of Miami, entered into the national system years before. The initial sample belonged to an unidentified man who had abducted a mother from a Presbyterian church preschool in southern Miami-Dade County and raped her multiple times in front of her toddler-aged son. Even the MOs lined up.

It was at this time that everyone officially began to refer to my assailant as a serial rapist, but with no further identifying information available, this man still lacked a face or a name to ease my fear. It was like having confirmation that a terrifying ghost exists somewhere near you, but not actually being able to defend yourself. You just have to wait on edge until he spooks you.

One very positive and immediate effect of tying the two DNA profiles to the same man was that my case stayed in the news. Communities are terrified of serial predators. Miami was on high alert, and residents in many of the traditionally safe and boring suburban areas were now starting to pay more attention to crime.

This man had obviously been living in the southern end of the county, hiding in plain sight for years, waiting to strike again. This reality prompted the creation of a countywide law enforcement task force to hunt for the newly minted "Daycare Rapist." It seemed like there were constant updates from the task force in the media. I was comforted by this since it meant people were still actively looking for him.

The task force's deep dive into prior sexual assault reports filed with the Miami-Dade police over the last five years resulted in the finding of two more cases with extremely similar MOs to mine. Both of these cases also took place in southern Miami-Dade County and had religious elements to them.

One involved a mom being abducted from a church preschool not far from where we were taken. She was brutally raped in front of her toddler-aged child in the year 2000. The other was of a mom and her toddler-aged son, who were carjacked in the parking lot of their pediatrician's office, driven to a church, and then taken to a similar location as I was and raped. This attack was full of religious rantings like the others. I was truly heartbroken when I learned that the victim in that case was eight months pregnant with her second child. Trust me when I say that this man is truly evil.

In total, there were now four cases being looked at. Two cases had DNA profiles, and all four had sketches of the attacker. So many of the details aligned. This man had committed one assault each year, starting in 1999. I was his fourth victim. Without resolution in my case, I am quite sure that I would not have been his last. It's worth noting that there was a little extra time in between his third and fourth assaults, which lined up with the story he told me about recently being in jail.

The police focused their search on many of the things he had told me during our time together. This included his statements about his recent incarceration, a traumatic childhood having a prostitute for a mom and an unknown father, and failing out of high school while living in a drug-infested neighborhood near downtown. I spent days helping detectives look through old high school yearbooks and recent parolee photos like a zombie, searching for my rapist with no success.

Less than three weeks after the assault, we got another surprising boost in the investigation. One of my detectives called and told me that John Walsh, from the popular TV show *America's Most Wanted*, had heard about our case and wanted to feature the serial rapes on his upcoming broadcast. John Walsh had strong ties to the South Florida law enforcement community due to his own son Adam's abduction and subsequent murder in the Fort Lauderdale area back in 1981.

The murder of Adam Walsh happened when I was in elementary school and is my first concrete memory of predatory evil in the world. The media images of six-year-old Adam in his red ball cap are etched in my mind forever. Fortunately for victims like me, John Walsh turned his grief into action and devoted the rest of his life to capturing elusive predators. Because of my admiration for the man and his mission, I agreed to appear on the show, although I was very nervous to reenter society in such a public way.

While I felt uncomfortable sharing details of the story with a national audience so soon after the attacks, I had promised the police to help in any way I could if they felt it would advance the investigation. I asked producers to show only a blacked-out silhouette of me while I was speaking to avoid being identified. My perpetrator had threatened that he would kill me if I alerted the police. I was pretty sure that calling for a widespread manhunt on national TV would definitely have filled him with a crazy level of homicidal rage.

Although his other victims did not speak on camera when we filmed, they were there with the police, answering questions and supporting me. I met each one of them, and we shared tears and words of encouragement. It felt like being in a twisted sisterhood and speaking a language no one else in the world would understand. That was the only time we were all together, but I will remember them always. The show aired the following week and resulted in a multitude of tips being called in. Unfortunately, none of them led to a break in the case.

16

Hunted and Found

INITIALLY, I FELT DEVASTATED that I had taken the risk of putting myself out there, only for it to result in no tangible progress. I felt like I was trying to catch a phantom who was forever beyond reach. What I couldn't see in those dark days, however, was how the seeds were being planted for my assailant's capture and my healing.

All of these years later, I am still in awe of John Walsh and the impact he has had on the criminal justice system as a dedicated father fighting for justice for other families. His involvement in our journey ultimately brought my family a semblance of closure.

Someday, I would like to thank him in person for what he did by choosing to get involved. Regardless of whether our paths cross again, his activism remains an inspiration for me as I try to advocate for others whose lives have been altered by violent crime.

As the weeks passed, I grew a little stronger mentally and was finally ready to face my fears and return home to the house I shared with Jamie and the kids. My in-laws had left, and Jamie needed to return to work. Most of the media and the chaos outside the house had faded away, and it was just the kids and me behind locked doors all day.

I will always appreciate my playgroup friends from church, who delivered meals and took my children out for playdates. We never would have survived the daily isolation without their kindness.

My mom was an incredible daily support too, sitting with me most days until Jamie got home from work because I was too afraid to be alone. When she couldn't be there, I hired babysitters to help out so I could get some rest. Being in a constant state of alert was exhausting, and my anxiety was making it impossible to sleep through the night.

The initial responding officer in my case would graciously come and sit in her squad car in front of the house while she caught up on paperwork sometimes, so that there was a visible police presence there to calm me. It's these little acts of support that made a huge difference in my ability to stay strong for my family.

My life, prior to the assaults, was dedicated to the care and well-being of my kids. But now, my life was centered around being completely present for my kids in a way that became absolutely all-consuming. I was in constant fear for their safety and concerned about their development.

I felt like I didn't even exist as a person outside of this mission. To help with their mental health, I was given a recommendation for our daughter to be seen by a skilled childhood psychologist named Dr. Susan Keeley, who, years before, had cofounded the Melissa Institute for Violence Prevention and Treatment. The institute happened to be named after a student from my old high school who was killed in a random act of extreme violence just before her college graduation in St. Louis, Missouri.

Just like with John Walsh and his show *America's Most Wanted*, my family was being helped along again in our time of need by an organization that was created from the grief of parents who understood profound loss and trauma and used that pain to help others.

Dr. Keeley beautifully said once about the creation of the institute, that Melissa's parents realized after their daughter's death that they, "had two choices: to curse the darkness, or to light a candle." They chose to light a candle. I think about those words all the time in my own advocacy.

At the Melissa Institute, Mia engaged in carefully designed play therapy to help with her extreme anxiety. After interacting with her therapist and hearing about the importance of early intervention, I learned that young children can retain trauma in their brains and bodies forever. It is stored within them with great intensity, and social science is now just beginning to grasp the magnitude of its damaging effects.

What is most cruel in situations like ours and many others is that, unlike adults, little kids have no context through which to make sense of sexual violence. They can feel its brutality as soon as they are exposed to it, but it requires a painful awakening over time to fill in the blanks with regard to the intimacy and indignity of it all.

I watched in wonder as my daughter, at only three years old, tried to make sense of the violence and devise ways to protect herself. For example, after being trapped in the van without access to a bathroom on the day we were abducted, she had no option but to soil herself. This was a big deal to her, as she had worked so hard to potty train and wear big girl pants. In fact, using the potty at school is why we went to the bookstore for a treat the day we were taken.

She devised a plan to only wear diapers from that point on, because in her brain, he could simply pop up and terrorize us again on any given day, so she needed to be prepared. It was something that made sense to her and was controllable. Thinking that young children are unaffected by what they see and experience just because they can't understand the totality of complex situations at the time is dangerously misguided.

Mia and I both went to therapy regularly as the weeks and then months dragged on. Friends and family helped take care of some of our basic needs while Jamie attempted to stay focused at work, and I struggled to find the energy to make it through the days. I basically stopped caring about my external appearance or whether or not the house was clean. I used that extra energy to obsess over identifying my rapist.

I was in constant touch with the detectives on my case, calling them for updates on leads regularly. When I wasn't calling them, my dad or husband would. Again, I have to say that I am grateful to have been raped in Miami. The victim-centered training given to officers in the sex crimes unit was effective and very much appreciated. I never felt like the police were annoyed by my calls or questions. They may have been, but they never let it show, calling me back promptly to reassure me that they were still hard at work on the case.

Thanksgiving crept up on us in November and felt distinctly different from how it had in the past. It lacked the festive Hallmark feel that we always looked forward to. Jamie and I had a special connection to the holiday because we got engaged seven years earlier at sunset on Thanksgiving Eve, celebrating afterward with friends and family at the church's annual service. There would be no church for us this year. It was too painful to go back. We spent the day with my parents and the kids, simply grateful to be alive. We took a walk outside and appreciated the cooler weather and the brightly shining sun on our skin. Thankfulness was expressed in the most simplistic way—smiles and prayers between loved ones. It was meaningful but different.

I started dreading the holiday season as soon as the calendar switched to December. Instead of Christmas shopping or planning a party, I spent my time hiding in my house searching for my Christmas spirit. It's weird how, when experiencing a crisis, the holidays shift from being a cause for celebration to events to be endured. The days were much shorter now, which compounded my depression.

I continued to communicate with the police, but there were no new leads. I sensed that the investigation may naturally slow down a bit until after the new year, and that made me insecure. Jamie and I decided that a change of scenery was what we needed, and we quickly planned a trip to his parents' house in Philadelphia. I knew that we would be physically safe there, and the kids would get to enjoy snow and the huge Christmas tree that my father-in-law had become famous for decorating every year.

The Pennsylvania trip was a good decision. There were definitely moments of true laughter and happiness where we were able to forget the heartache back home. The most memorable part of the vacation for me was Christmas morning.

I had stopped wearing my wedding rings immediately after the incident because they reminded me of the fake wedding I had been forced into with my rapist and how he had rubbed the once-cherished rings all over his cruel body.

On Christmas morning, I stumbled out of bed and into the living room, where I found that Jamie had tied a tiny satin bag onto one of the beautifully trimmed branches in the center of the tree. In the bag were my original wedding rings, now reforged and made new. In addition to the diamond solitaire of the engagement ring, he had two new, smaller diamonds placed on each side—a beautiful symbol of our marriage and the lives of our children. It was perfect, and I felt whole again when Jamie placed the rings on my finger.

In fact, it all felt so good that I grew hesitant about returning home. Jamie had to go back to Miami for work, but the kids and I decided to stay in Pennsylvania a little bit longer. It was during this period that I realized that the best thing for our family's well-being may be to move out of Miami. This was a thought that I previously never would have allowed to enter my mind. One night, the thought of moving gnawed at me so intensely that I got onto the internet in my in-laws' freezing basement and began researching new places where we could start over. I would miss my parents, my house, and our community with all of my heart, but I realized I was dying inside trying to feel safe again in a place where my rapist was running free.

Jamie understood my feelings, and we started daydreaming together about where we might go. We knew that being near family was an asset with kids, so having a connection to someone close to where we moved was important.

His family was from the Northeast; however, Jamie realized that he had been in Florida for so long that he had no desire to return to the cold. This fact also meant moving closer to my extended family in Iowa was off the table. His professional licensing was in Florida, so that was something to take into consideration, since only one of us would be working for a while.

If we were to stay in Florida, though, it needed to be at least two hours away from Miami for it to feel like any real change of place. Proximity to the coast was something we both wanted too. Eventually, our checklist narrowed down our workable options to one city: Jupiter, FL.

The only thing that I knew about Jupiter growing up was that it was a town north of Miami with a very funny name. I learned a lot more about it, though, after getting to know my husband's college roommate and his wife. I was introduced to both of them during Jamie's senior year of college and loved them immediately.

Although his college was up in Northeastern Pennsylvania, his roommate was originally from Jupiter. He and his wife moved back to his hometown after he finished graduate school, and we always loved road tripping to the quiet town to visit them.

As a couple, we went through all of our milestones together in our 20s, like engagements, weddings, and hunting for our first homes. They were the first people we told when we found out I was pregnant. In fact, we delivered the news in the living room of their first house, which is only about one and a half miles from where we live now.

That day, they told us that they were pregnant too. Our daughters were born just ten days apart. A couple of years later, we both had sons just three months apart. They were the first friends Jamie called on the night of the attack. It would be like living near family.

While the decision to move was made and steadily gaining momentum in our minds, the timetable for leaving Miami was not yet set. There was still too much going on in the hunt for our assailant, and we didn't want to introduce another abrupt change into the children's lives. Unbeknownst to us, things were happening with our abductor in mid-January that would crack the case wide open. It all started with a domestic violence arrest.

On a cold night down in Homestead, our abductor was staying in a motel room with his pregnant girlfriend, who also happened to be the mother of his two-year-old son. A fight broke out between them that turned physical, and a bystander called the police. When the police arrived, they arrested the man and took him to the Homestead police station. Once there, he was booked on the charge of felony battery on a pregnant woman.

He was at the police station for hours that night while details of the domestic assault and his identifying information were collected. He was eventually released from custody and slithered back into the arms of his girlfriend, but the charges against him remained.

A few weeks later, we were in our house having dinner when we heard the sounds of police sirens in the distance. A little bit later, we heard the sounds of a helicopter flying over our neighborhood; it was circling around with the spotlight on. The commotion made me very anxious, but we pretended not to notice and went about our nighttime ritual.

The relative calm inside the house was shattered when, sometime after 10 p.m., there was a loud knock on our front door. It was startling, like a telephone ringing in the dead of night. Jamie saw a police car through the window and opened the front door to find two officers waiting on our porch. They apologized for the late, unannounced visit and then asked to speak with me.

I made sure the kids were safely sound asleep in their rooms and then entered the living room to greet them, visibly shaken. I noticed that they had a file folder in their hands. Without any mention of the police activity that had been going on in the area all evening, they asked me if I thought that I could identify the man who had raped me. Obviously, there must have been a substantial break in the case if they were going to show me photos of a presumed suspect.

I said that I thought I could. Before they showed me the lineup of pictures, they repeatedly told me that I had to be 100 percent sure of the identity. If I had even the slightest doubt, I would have to decline making a positive ID.

I looked closely at each of the faces. They all seemed so ordinary and nonthreatening. The man I was looking for had evil behind his eyes. He was red in the face, screaming at me and threatening me, telling me that my kids were going to watch me die. He was a sweaty, angry mess of a human. None of the men in the lineup radiated that type of unhinged fury.

I ended up ruling out a few of them fairly quickly. The officers had me write the word "no" in the bottom corner of the photos. There were two pictures that gave me pause at first, and after closer examination, I felt that one of them really resembled him. The officers continued to repeat that I should not make the positive ID unless I was 100 percent sure that it was the right guy. I was quite sure that it was him, but 100 percent was a leap that I just couldn't make in my heart.

The last thing I wanted to do was accuse an innocent man and have the real criminal still out in the community. I initialized "no" at the bottom of each photo, and the police left my home. I went to sleep extremely frustrated that night.

Later, the next morning, I received a call from my lead detective telling me that my perpetrator had been in the photo lineup I was shown the night before. He had been positively identified through DNA and a partial fingerprint in one of the other cases. I was stunned. Suddenly, my rapist had an actual identity. What happened next in this story convinced me, beyond any shadow of a doubt, that miracles are real.

The day of the manhunt and the late-night knock on my door, the Miami-Dade crime lab finished processing the evidence from the random domestic violence arrest that occurred in Homestead at the end of January. The task force that was assembled shortly after my assault had been taking voluntary DNA swabs and making special note of any arrestees who resembled my sketch of the "Daycare Rapist." As you might imagine, over a few months' time, the police lab had a large stack of DNA to work through. Fortunately for me, Miami-Dade was not experiencing a backlog like other areas in the country and was staying on top of its samples.

On the date officers came to my house with the photo lineup, the evidence from the January domestic violence case had been run through the national DNA database earlier in the day and matched with another sample that was already in the system from a similar rape in 2000. That rape was linked to mine early on in the investigation, but there was no name attached to the perpetrator. Now that forensic evidence from the domestic violence and sexual violence cases were connected, though, police could positively identify the "Daycare Rapist." My predator had a name, at last. It was Michael Thomas Seibert. When the identity was confirmed that day, it was only released to a handful of people within law enforcement. They kept the circle very small and started crafting a strategic way to capture him before disseminating the information to the general public, in case he ran.

One of the few people informed of my rapist's identity was the analyst who ran the original DNA sample from my Tinkerbell T-shirt. I already thought of her as my angel, and now she would solidify her status further.

It had been an eventful day at work, and that night, she decided to pick up fast food for dinner. While she was waiting for her food at the drive-thru window of a random Burger King, Michael Seibert happened to be standing at the register inside with his arm around his pregnant girlfriend and their two-year-old son.

At the time, Miami had a metropolitan area of over five million people. It is absolutely inconceivable to me that one of only a handful of people in the entire world who knew my attacker's identity that night happened to notice him through a window at a fast-food restaurant.

The whistleblower ended up being my very own analyst Lisbeth Colon, who had already gone above and beyond in the case by finding the small mixed sample of DNA on my Tinkerbell T-shirt. Divine intervention is the only way I can rationalize this happening. To say it was a miracle almost feels like an understatement.

Upon seeing him at the Burger King, the analyst immediately called 9-1-1, and police cars swarmed the location. Incredibly, Seibert was able to evade the cavalry of officers and escape the perimeter they set up. He ran out of the restaurant and through private yards, hiding under bridges and hopping on buses, eventually fleeing the area.

When I was informed of Michael Seibert's identity the next day, I felt both relieved and frightened. I was relieved because the monster now had a name and face that I could clearly identify. Others would hopefully be able to aid in the search more effectively now that he was a known suspect.

I was frightened, though, because he was still out there and might come back to kill us like he promised. He was surely desperate, and his threats were embedded so deeply in my psyche that I convinced myself that we were more vulnerable than ever. I was disgusted by how normal he looked in the picture.

Immediately, all levels of law enforcement in the state went public with his photograph. John Walsh did another episode about him on *America's Most Wanted*, this time with his name and photograph.

The whole country was now looking for Michael Thomas Seibert, and I grew cautiously optimistic that he would be found quickly.

Weeks passed, however, and no news or information about credible sightings came into the call centers. I started to lose hope again, and my nightmares intensified. Now, when I had bad dreams, there was a face attached to the devil inside my head.

I was back to not sleeping at all and felt like a zombie during the day. When I would occasionally feel brave enough to leave my house, I ran into police flyers hung up all over town with his image on them. I felt like I couldn't escape his presence.

Seeing his face everywhere started wearing out my friends and family too. Some of them volunteered to help police pass out flyers and took them to supermarkets, parks, restaurants, and "adult establishments" down in the southern part of the county, in and around Homestead.

Business owners recognized him as a frequent patron and said that he seemed, as many successful predators do, like a "normal" guy. The manager at a dockside restaurant where we had dined a few times recognized him from a recent visit. Seibert was clearly a resident of the area and knew it well, although he had not been seen in the last few weeks.

My desire to move away from the neighborhood that I adored intensified. He could still be close by, and no amount of love for my home or my community could dampen my fear of him. I contacted a realtor friend and started to go over our listing options.

I woke up every day that spring like it was Groundhog Day. I threw water on my face, ran a brush through my hair, and put on my clothes just in case I had to flee the premises. I would clean up around the house, wait for my mom to come sit with me, and watch the kids play inside. While my mom was there, I called my detectives and others on the task force to check for developments.

I routinely gazed out of the windows around my house, searching for him in the bushes and on the streets. After being on heightened alert for hours and trying to mask my depression, I would often take an afternoon nap until dinner. It didn't even feel like I was living anymore. I was just waking up and breathing, existing solely to catch Michael Seibert and protect my children.

The highlight of most days was looking online at homes in new communities where we could rebuild our lives. Deep down, I dreaded leaving the place I loved so much, but I knew that to save myself mentally, we had to go. On March 25, a for sale sign was placed in our front yard. I sobbed.

After a fitful night of sleep, I jumped into the shower the next morning, determined to make something productive out of the day. As I stood under the steady stream of water, I suddenly heard yelling at the other end of the house. It was loud and working its way closer to me. Jamie soon bounced into the bathroom and began shouting, "Julie, they caught him! They caught Seibert! Sweetie, it's over!"

He stepped completely into the shower and held me while I collapsed, trying to process the news. My next breaths felt lighter than they had in months. Like turning on a light switch, everything around me suddenly looked brighter and less frightening. I felt new hope rush into me and immediately went to hug the kids.

17

After the Capture

CONVERSATIONS WITH MY DETECTIVES and the task force representatives confirmed what Jamie had told me. In the early morning hours of March 26, in New Smyrna Beach, FL, Michael Thomas Seibert was captured while sleeping in a car on the side of the road. He was taken into custody by local officers who recognized his face from *America's Most Wanted* and statewide police bulletins.

My detectives in Miami informed me that Seibert had been arrested and was being extradited back to Miami-Dade County for arraignment. He was currently en route with Detective KL, the very first sex crimes officer I met six months earlier, and a key member of the task force. The drive back to Miami would take nearly four hours.

What a weird day March 26, 2003, had been already. At this point, it was only around noon, and I was reeling from all of the information being thrown at me. I was used to quiet days, existing in fear with my head on a swivel, looking for him. And now—this.

Jamie took the kids to my mom and dad's house before the action around our home started to get more intense. My phone was ringing off the hook while police cars and the media were once again parked in front of the house. My heart was racing from all of the excitement. The news that filtered in from my detectives throughout the day seemed almost too bizarre to be true. I wanted all of the details. I needed to know everything about the evil man whose body had once moved inside of me.

The first thing I learned about him was something that came as no surprise: he was a pathological liar. He intended to throw everyone involved in the investigation off his trail from the start. He crafted elaborate details of a fake life that differed from his real one in every way. To begin with, there had been no prison time for Seibert—not even an arrest in his backstory. He was an ordinary, white, non-Hispanic guy who was about nine years older than me (born in 1962). He grew up in a middle-class neighborhood and attended my rival high school, located less than ten miles from the site of our abduction. He had never lived on the streets of inner-city Miami. Rather, this predator grew up in a nice area of suburban Miami and, for a short time, lived in an affluent suburb of northern Virginia close to Washington, DC.

I think what stunned me most were the terrible lies Seibert told about his family situation, with the sole intention of manipulating my view of him. There was no drug-addicted prostitute mother or absentee father in his history. In fact, when police found him, he was sleeping in a car just blocks from his own parents' home in New Smyrna Beach, FL. His mom was a former secretary at a local Presbyterian church in Miami, and his dad was a retired federal agent with Alcohol, Tobacco, Firearms, and Explosives (ATF), who had also served with the United States Secret Service for multiple presidents. Michael Seibert was the complete opposite of a homeless drifter or a hardened criminal. He had parents who had been married for decades, as well as a brother and a sister, and he had never been in trouble with the law. His upbringing defied all of the stereotypes that I had attributed to his violent nature. The most disturbing revelation of all, however, was that Seibert himself was the father of five children. One of his children, whose mother was the victim in his domestic violence arrest, was born just days before his capture.

Late that afternoon, I switched places with Jamie, and he brought the children back to our house. I went to my parents' home that night so I could watch the news coverage of his capture. I sat on the couch in front of the television with my dad while my mom was in the back of the house. As soon as the story about my rapist's arrest came on the news, I started to scream and cry uncontrollably.

It was mind-blowing to me that while he was being escorted into the Miami-Dade police station, he stopped for a minute to address reporters. When he started running his mouth, I yelled, "It's him! It's him! That's the voice! See, the way he is walking? That's the swagger I saw after he fled the van!"

Upon hearing my screams, my mom rushed into the room and hugged me tightly while I explained to her that hearing the man on the screen talk and seeing him move in three dimensions gave me absolute certainty that the police had the right guy.

The freedom I suddenly felt was intense. For months, I had been existing in the shadows, figuratively chained to a man whom I felt would kill my family at any moment. But now, with his identity known and his power gone, I started to feel like I was living in a brand-new body.

I spent the next few days and weeks crying out of sheer relief, walking around my neighborhood with my face in the sunshine, and welcoming friends into my home without fearing they would be in danger. While I still felt inherently different as a person, life around me started to regain its color for the first time in six months. I still felt numb and awkward, but grateful that I no longer had to live in paralyzing fear.

Shortly after the arrest, we moved two hours north to Palm Beach County, FL. I thought about taking the house off the market when Seibert was captured and staying put, but I knew that I would never feel entirely safe. I still felt so vulnerable and wasn't sure if I would ever be able to shake that feeling if we stayed.

The local streets, parks, and especially my church had too many bad memories associated with them now, and we needed to rebuild our lives in a new place that felt safe. My children deserved that opportunity.

Moving provided a good diversion from my constant thoughts about the crime, but it did not stop me from obsessing over Michael Seibert, the man. I kept in close touch with the law enforcement officers who had worked on my case in Miami, even after the arrest, learning everything I could about him and his history.

I eventually met the state attorney down in Miami who would be prosecuting my case, as well as his team of advocates and witness coordinators. Once we had established a basic relationship, I started calling them several times a week to stay on top of the details of the impending trial. It seemed like things were beginning to move toward closure. Hope seemed possible.

In hindsight, *moving* may be too strong a verb to describe the criminal justice process at that point. Inching towards closure—or hanging in suspended animation—is probably more accurate. Depositions were taken of all the victims in the case, but communication was not quite as reliable or constant as it had been with law enforcement. The state attorney's office had a high rate of employee turnover, and strong relationships were much harder for me to build. The attorney was nice and competent, but I felt disconnected from the process.

Eventually, my attorney moved on from working for the state and took a position in a private practice. I was promptly assigned a new attorney for my criminal trial, but the exact same thing happened with them. It became a pattern. Just as I would build up some level of trust, the assigned prosecutor would leave, and we would be back to square one. Nearly two years post-arrest, I still didn't feel very confident that my case would ever see the inside of a courtroom. I was losing my confidence that anyone was truly committed to fighting for my family.

The biggest frustrations came, however, with the defense counsel. Seibert's assigned representation changed six different times before he settled on an attorney. During the years that this was happening, the ever-spinning carousel of lawyers caused constant disruption in our everyday lives with more depositions and continuances.

We could never schedule vacations or make concrete plans because the trial date constantly shifted. I was unable to go back to work due to my extreme anxiety, PTSD, and the ever-present uncertainty of when the trial would start. Before I became acquainted with the justice system, I had no idea that victims had to wait so long to get their day in court. The process felt like it strongly favored the accused, while the victim continued to fight for any semblance of control.

I used these frustrating years to grow more familiar with our new community in Jupiter, FL. It was difficult for me to feel like it was "home," since my mind and heart were still in Miami. I felt like I was split between two places. I spent all of my free time at my son's and daughter's elementary school and was involved in their extracurricular activities to help them, and myself feel more secure in our new environment. It was a good distraction.

All day, I would try to put on a brave face for the kids and internalize my sadness so they wouldn't feel the heaviness of the situation. At night, I would stay up late and ruminate over the things I had been hiding from in the daylight. I was exhausted. Unfortunately, I know my children could sense it on some level.

Only our friends from college who lived in Jupiter and our family really knew why we relocated to the quiet suburb of West Palm Beach. In the very beginning, aside from the kids' teachers, we kept most of the information about our move private and didn't discuss it extensively with neighbors or new friends. It's hard enough to make friends when you are an adult without announcing that you are the "rape family" from Miami.

Keeping our circumstances quiet worked out well at the start, but soon the loneliness of not having people to vent to about our situation grew heavy. I missed my friends from home and my therapist. I struggled to connect with people on an authentic level because my depression worsened, and I felt like I was constantly wearing a mask.

Jamie found a new therapist for me, which helped, but the adjustment to our new life took time. Already in these early years after the crime, I started to experience a sense of profound loss. This feeling would grow over the course of the next decade until I found a way to reframe my pain.

In 2004, my luck began to change, and I began to feel more hopeful that justice might finally happen for us. My case had been assigned to a brilliant young prosecutor named Laura Adams, who had the tenacity of a bulldog. She was a strong communicator and, from day one, made me feel like our case was the only thing that mattered to her. She became an empathetic ear, a great source of procedural information, and, most importantly, my most fervent cheerleader.

She connected me with compassionate advocates at the State Attorney's Office who could provide comfort and advice when multiple continuance notifications would show up in my mailbox. I can still hear her talking me down off the ledge after the numerous delays by saying phrases like, "It will all be worth it in the end," "Let's make sure we give him no grounds to appeal when we win," and "Just keep holding on."

I ended up needing every ounce of strength and reassurance she could give me. A plea deal was proposed shortly after she took over my case that would send Seibert to jail for thirty years for all four of the rapes connected to him. When I was contacted about the deal, my heart broke. There was no way that I could ever agree to that plea.

Michael Seibert would be out of prison before he was seventy-five years old and free to hurt us again. He could very well be healthy enough and full of enough rage towards me that he could come back and do serious harm to our family. I had repeatedly vowed to everyone in my home that he would never walk the earth again while any of us were still alive.

It was that promise that motivated me to keep fighting on my hardest days. His other victims agreed to the plea, most likely to spare themselves the pain of facing him at trial or the risk of his being acquitted. I simply could not.

I shared my concerns with Laura Adams, and she thankfully did not pressure me to take the deal. When I told her I wanted my day in court, she rolled up her sleeves and said, "We'd better get to work." She assured me that my case alone could put him away for life and that she had complete confidence in the evidence and the witnesses. She warned me that going to trial is always risky, but assured me it would be worth it if I had the stamina.

Her encouragement meant everything to me and felt like rocket fuel, powering me towards the justice I so deeply craved. It might take a couple more years to see justice, and it would be tedious work. But she believed in the mission—and that belief was enough to keep me standing.

18

The Trial of Truth

SEIBERT WAS UNHAPPY WITH my decision to reject the deal. During the months that followed, I read bits of information that indicated he was angry with me and wanted to know my location. I felt sick every day and, at times, I doubted my decision to take him to trial. I am sure the people around me thought I was crazy for being so frightened of a man who spent his days in solitary confinement within a high-security jail. From the outside, my fear must have looked irrational. Those people, however, had never been in Seibert's presence.

He was a predatory chameleon, intent on being whoever he needed to be to manipulate a situation. He was violent and very determined to take what he wanted. His possible escape filled my nightmares. Fear did not obey logic. Was I really strong enough to keep going when things got more intense? Many days, I wrestled with doubt.

I coped with my increasing anxiety by keeping in constant communication with my contacts in the justice system. They encouraged me and said that I was doing the right thing, even if it felt impossible. I ramped up my visits to my psychologist and leaned hard on my family. I felt guilty at times, though, for what my emotions were triggering inside of them.

I was so nervous he would get out and hurt my kids that I practically lived at the elementary school as a volunteer. I convinced myself that as long as I was not at home alone and I was in close proximity to my kids, we would all be safer. Vigilance became my coping mechanism. The months all ran together, and years passed. I held on to whatever hope I could muster that this would all eventually end, and I could go back to who I was before.

Relief came almost four years after the date of our abduction. Finally, everything was ready to go for trial in October of 2006. I was on pins and needles that it would be cancelled again, right up until the last minute. My in-laws flew in from Pennsylvania to stay with the children while I went to Miami for the duration of the trial. Jamie drove back and forth between locations, trying to be there for all of us.

The kids knew I was gone, trying to keep the "bad man" in jail forever. I learned firsthand that children absorb the stress of their parents, even if they can't articulate precisely why they are sad or frightened. I am grateful that they had their aunt, uncle, and grandparents to make them feel secure. I remember kissing their sweet little faces when I left the house the night before the trial. Their hugs reminded me of why I took up this fight.

Halloween morning, I woke up in my childhood bedroom. It felt like a full-circle moment being in that sacred space again. It had been exactly four years and two weeks since the day my life, once again, changed forever. I remember how desperate I felt running into my parents' house after the rapes that day. Now, four years later, I was in the same spot—empowered to fight for justice and reclaim my life.

My body trembled as I got ready. Still, I kept moving. As silly as it sounds, I flashed back to my high school debate days when I would put on a suit and head out to a tournament, confident in my arguments. I clung to my faith and reminded myself that God had been present with me through all of my traumas and preserved my spirit even when I thought I couldn't go on. He endowed me with courage and inner strength, and the gifts of speech and veracity. I left my house ready for battle.

I made small talk in the car with my parents as we drove downtown to the courthouse. It was not lost on any of us that it was across the street from Jackson Memorial Hospital and the rape crisis center where the journey began. The geography alone felt symbolic.

As the outcry witness, my mom was the first person to take the stand. My dad was in the courtroom as well, and I was assigned to a room away from the proceedings with an advocate to help me manage my emotions. I felt so helpless— not in my own ability to face my attacker, but helpless to help my loved ones.

While my immediate family knew many of the graphic details of the crime, I tried to shield them from the most disturbing parts. Now, my parents were sitting in a room where everything was going to come to light, just yards from the man who almost killed their daughter and grandchildren. I wanted to take that hurt away from them.

Following the attorney's opening statements, my mom kicked off the trial with her brutal account of what happened on October 16, 2002, when I arrived screaming at their home. She bravely faced down Michael Seibert, who sat at a nearby table with his attorney.

I heard from the witness coordinator that my mom's recollection of the details that day, especially her account of how traumatized my children were, was crystal clear. She was incredibly strong in the presence of evil. I will be forever proud of her grit and composure in that terrible situation. I appreciate the immense love she has in her heart that enabled her to overcome her fear.

I was also informed by the witness coordinator that Seibert's family was present and sitting in the row directly behind him. His father was dressed in his uniform, and his mom and brother looked like characters out of a Hallmark movie. They appeared picture perfect. It was also relayed to me that the defendant, my real-life monster, was nicely dressed in a jacket and tie with a cleanly shaven face and calm demeanor. Michael Seibert must have looked to others in the courtroom like any other suburban family man. He definitely was a master of disguise.

Day one was exhausting for my parents in the courtroom and for Jamie and me, who were cloistered away. I was informed that I would be the last witness in the trial and, therefore, could not be present in the courtroom during the testimonies of anyone else. I could be in the courthouse with my advocate, but I was not permitted to listen in.

Sleep was extremely elusive for me that night. As confident as I was in my decision to go to trial and in the power of the evidence, there was a tiny part of me that wondered if I had enough emotional strength inside of me to go the distance. I knew there would be many more days of torturous testimony by others ahead.

I felt the familiar sensation of losing control that I had grown accustomed to throughout both the physical rape and the judicial process. Would the witnesses remember the case with clarity after all these years? Would they be able to convey the details of that horrible night and the hunt that followed with the level of intensity required to convict this man beyond a reasonable doubt?

His multiple defense attorneys had intentionally caused delays in the process over the years for their client's benefit. People naturally have difficulty remembering details over time, and witnesses can become less reliable. Would the defense strategy work? My soul finally comprehended the risk of it all.

From the beginning, my dad was a pillar of strength, a constant fixture in the courtroom. He represented our family day after day, no matter how graphic or technical the testimony was. I can't imagine how difficult that must have been for him to hear the details and how much strength was required to see Michael Seibert and his family over and over again. I felt retraumatized by the courtroom process, but felt even worse for my family, who had to go through it all over again too.

Fortunately, the case was strong, and the people who treated me and handled the evidence in my case came through with flying colors. While the defense attempted to rip apart the testimony of the nurses, officers, and DNA experts, each witness stood firm and recounted their part in the journey with extreme professionalism.

His defense was all over the place and seemed to shift strategy with each new revelation to the jury. In reading the transcripts from the trial, it is clear to me that each person who was called to give testimony was well-trained. Notes from law enforcement and the medical professionals at the RCC were expertly detailed and allowed the jury to hear concise accounts of my physical and emotional state in the immediate aftermath. I am forever grateful to every person who came in contact with me that horrible night for their attention to detail and ability to give unwavering testimony. I never knew how important this would be until my pursuit of justice depended on it.

The defense had their work cut out for them, and during opening statements and cross-examination, chose to rely on societal stereotypes about where rapists come from and what they look like. His team focused on Michael Seibert's family background, the notion that he was a father and community volunteer, and how ridiculously far-fetched my story seemed. Seibert was a family man and didn't need to rape anyone. After all, he didn't look like a violent felon, so it must not be him. I prayed in earnest that the jury would be able to see past what was on display and acknowledge his capacity for evil.

In terms of his identity, I will be forever indebted to the science of DNA and my specific analyst for informing the world that the normal-looking man standing trial was, in fact, a violent predator. No matter how you dress him up or what decent people you surround him with, Michael Seibert is a rapist and a sadist. His "genetic fingerprint" proved that.

Despite all of his efforts to erase the evidence during the assault, he had failed. This serial rapist finally made a huge, yet microscopic, mistake. It invalidated all of the defense claims that Seibert had never seen or been with me before. The scientific proof was an irrefutable witness.

I am fortunate that my analyst tested the shirt where the sample was found instead of just shutting the testing down after my rape kit contained no biological evidence. I am still blown away by the fact that she was the person who spotted Michael Seibert at the Burger King and called 9-1-1. I am most grateful, though, for her testimony in the courtroom.

It is difficult for common citizens on a jury to understand the complexities of DNA. It takes a very professional analyst to be able to explain the scientific nuances and complex probabilities to a group of laypeople who are charged with deciding someone's guilt or innocence.

The defense tried to say the DNA was faulty, contaminated, and not definitively his. They erroneously claimed that the lab may have made mistakes. They tried very hard to weave skepticism into the most compelling evidence that linked him to the crime. When she took the stand, my analyst was confident and could explain, with clarity, why it was him, beyond any reasonable doubt.

Law enforcement showed up in force to testify about the reports generated the night of the crime, as well as about the hunt and eventual capture of the defendant. Despite the defense constantly chirping that it was not Michael Seibert who committed the crimes, the officers' notes were one more nail in his coffin. Detective KL, in particular, gave incredibly compelling testimony about conversations that happened between him and the defendant after Seibert's arrest in New Smyrna Beach, FL.

After basically confessing to the crime during his extradition to Miami and while in the initial custody of Miami-Dade law enforcement detectives from the task force, Seibert used his one phone call to phone his father for advice. Despite spending his adult life dedicated to upholding ideals of law enforcement at the federal level, Michael Seibert's father chose to act as his son's advocate and advised him not to sign a sworn statement. Seibert had been fully Mirandaized, but the spontaneous talks were not recorded or videoed. Without the sworn statement, there was no verbatim confession that was admissible in trial. Instead, jurors had to weigh the veracity of Detective KL's notes and recollection of the conversations during his testimony.

In hindsight, the information contained in Detective KL's testimony about the horrific Seibert discussions was both validating and maddening to me. Seibert described how he successfully hunted vulnerable women like me for years and how his actions weren't about sex, but rather centered around control and humiliation of his victims.

He talked extensively about what happened to me and emphasized that he did not target me in advance. Rather, during his surveillance of the church parking lot that day, he saw me talking to a friend and juggling kids. He mentioned that I was small in stature and looked disorganized and distracted. He laughed when he recounted to the detective how dangerous it was for women to drive minivans. He claimed that he warned his pregnant girlfriend of this fact repeatedly.

What bothered me the most about his statements was his repeated claims that he had very little interaction with my children during the abduction. Seibert said that while the kids' involvement was important in order to force my compliance with his sexual demands, he didn't view them as victims. He insisted that he did not hurt or threaten them at all.

He lied, saying he looked out for their well-being the whole time, even stopping to make sure they were securely buckled into their car seats before he raped me. This felt like a shot through my heart since nothing could be farther from the truth. He, in fact, delighted in the power of life and death that he had over my daughter and relished her fear. The more my children cried, the more empowered he became.

According to the detective's testimony, Seibert went so far as to emphatically declare that he loved children and would kill someone if they did the kinds of things he was accused of in front of his own kids. Michael Seibert is truly a master of deception and a self-aggrandized monster who believed in his own noble brilliance as a criminal.

The testimony from Detective KL was lengthy, lending further insight into the mindset of the perpetrator. Seibert's self-serving lies during his conversation with law enforcement included his account that he only assaulted me once after he abducted us. As the victim of his brutal assaults, it felt like he was trying to painfully minimize the damage that he had done. By saying that he only raped me once, he was trying to infer that it was just a lapse of judgment and something he did in a manic state.

He also claimed that he was on a "suicide mission" and knew from the outset that he had dripped DNA evidence onto my shirt, saying he wanted to be caught. The prolific serial rapist was too full of pride to admit that he had actually made a mistake and been outsmarted by technology and science. He peppered his narrative with facts about his crimes against us, as well as his previous victims, with the perfect amount of bravado to leave him feeling that he had always been the one in control.

Finally, after a week of being cloistered away in a side room with an advocate, it was my turn to take the stand. I felt viscerally ill when I stepped into the courtroom to testify. I first locked eyes with my husband, who was in the public gallery, and with my father, who sat next to him. They were flanked by security. I assume this was to help control any reactions they might have during my testimony. I took great comfort in their presence and in the relationship that I had developed with my prosecutor. I trusted her implicitly and knew that she would handle what was coming with compassion and professionalism.

I had spoken in front of large groups of people many times in my past and never found it difficult to find the words to express myself or bolster an argument. On this day, though, the stakes were much higher than at any other time in my life. One look at the defendant and my whole brain turned to mush, and I felt like I was literally back in my van, fighting for my life. He was there, in front of me, staring holes right through me. I was, once again, sitting just feet from pure evil. I prayed to God to give me the strength to speak the truth.

No one can really prepare you for what it is like to come face-to-face with the monster who tried to violently destroy your family. While I tried not to look at him, my body sensed his overwhelming presence with every breath. Within moments of taking the stand, I realized I was going to have to tap into a warrior mindset if I was going to survive.

I resolved in my heart that this would be the final round of the fight he started four years earlier. I was tired and scared and yet resolved to channel all of my fear, desperation, and the love I carried for my children into one final knockout punch. I would need divine empowerment to deliver the blow.

The whole experience was both terrifying and liberating. I felt deeply humiliated describing what my children and I endured that day, especially the graphic details about the four sexual assaults. He was seated across from me, and I could see the delight in his eyes as I recounted the pain and torture he inflicted on me and the effect his actions had on my children, who were forced to watch.

At one point in my testimony, I grew so emotional that I asked the court if I could take a break. My mind went into sensory overload as if the crime was happening again in real time. Quickly, I retreated from the witness stand and vomited into a nearby waste can.

In addition to the disturbing physical response I was having, I was simultaneously embarrassed that a courtroom full of strangers, my precious family, and the media now knew the vivid details of the disgusting acts I participated in to keep my children alive. I felt gross and ashamed by those actions, publicly exposed with my vulnerability on display for the world.

Aside from my therapist and the attorney, I had never shared the worst parts of the story with anyone in my life for fear of traumatizing them further and making them even sadder. Now, however, I couldn't hide what happened from anyone, including myself. That realization knocked the wind out of me, and I felt like I hit rock bottom—figuratively naked and very much afraid. There was nothing to lose and no place lower to fall. The truth had cost me everything, but it had also given me back my voice.

Once I survived reliving the horror of the original day, I instantly started to experience a weird sense of freedom that grew moment by moment. Exposing myself and letting others hear my truth was painful but cathartic. With the most graphic parts of my testimony behind me, I felt a renewed sense of purpose. My soul began to rise.

I thought about why I originally declined the plea deal and pressed to go to trial. I needed to be a soldier in that courtroom—disciplined, grounded, and decidedly unafraid of him anymore. The mission to keep him locked up forever depended on the power of my words to slay him so he couldn't harm anyone ever again. This was the final battle.

I stood strong when cross-examined by his defense and did not crumble when they tried to question my credibility or motives. Admittedly, though, it is ridiculously hard to restrain oneself when you are being cast as a liar and a desperate housewife, someone fabricating the events of a violent crime and accusing an innocent man.

It is also difficult to be cross-examined by a merciless defense attorney about the true extent of the psychological damage your family suffered. Seibert's lawyer painted a superficial picture of me as a woman whose life had only improved over the intervening years, having moved to the peaceful town of Jupiter, FL, where I had a nice home.

He mocked my countenance, saying I was pleasant and smiled too often for someone who was severely traumatized. The defense attorney implied through his questioning that any family dysfunction appeared to be minimal, and therefore, the supposed crime must not have been that bad. He claimed our lives had simply gotten better since we moved away from Miami.

I started to feel physically sick again, like I had been punched in the gut. This attorney didn't care about the pain I hid every single day for four years, silencing my tears so that my children and my husband would not see my heart breaking out loud. The jury never heard about the times I wished Michael Seibert had gone ahead and killed me. They didn't know that on my worst days, his leaving me alive to suffer the painful flashbacks and crushed dreams felt more cruel than death itself.

I wanted to cry out and beg the jury to listen to the details of my suffering, but the defense's questions were purposefully designed to minimize the damage done to me. This was not a search for truth; it was a performance meant to make my suffering invisible.

When the excruciating cross-examination was over, the State of Florida rested its case. I felt emotionally battered but, thankfully, not defeated. Surprisingly, the defense rested immediately. They called no witnesses. They offered no alibi. Michael Seibert did not take the stand in his own defense. I was stunned. I should have felt nothing but relief at that moment, but instead I found myself outraged.

Deep down, I was hoping that the trial process would give me answers—a motive or the reasoning behind why he was capable of such extreme violence. My mind needed to be given some kind of excuse for his behavior so that I didn't have to face the cold reality that some people are simply the embodiment of evil. Instead, the defense offered nothing, only the same hollow insistence that Seibert was not the perpetrator of any crime against me.

19

Reasonable Doubt

BY THE TIME CLOSING arguments arrived, the trial no longer felt like a legal proceeding. It felt personal. Every detail, every witness, every word spoken about that day had been weighed, twisted, and contested. Now it would come down to one final question: whether the jury would believe me.

There would be no more testimony. No more evidence. No more chances to clarify or correct. The court adjourned for the weekend. Monday morning, the judge thanked the jurors for their service, and the lawyers each made their closing statements.

After giving the jury detailed instructions about what the state needed to prove in order to return a guilty verdict against Michael Seibert, State Attorney Laura Adams pleaded with them to look at the totality of the evidence against the defendant.

She asked them to recall the lengthy testimonies of multiple law enforcement officers, medical personnel, and DNA experts who were mobilized to help us after the kidnappings and rapes.

She highlighted his domestic violence arrest and how the identifying information collected in that case scientifically linked him to mine.

She pointed out his consciousness of guilt when he fled from the Burger King and the incriminating statements he made to Detective KL after he was finally taken into custody weeks later.

The State confidently and methodically connected the physical, testimonial, and circumstantial evidence in the case and asked the jury—plainly and rationally—to return a guilty verdict on each of the eight major charges they were asked to consider.

Then it was the defense's turn.

The defense came out swinging and did its best to cast a pall of uncertainty over all of the evidence. After all, the jury only needed to be a little skeptical in order to amass enough reasonable doubt to acquit the defendant.

The defense attorney insisted that Michael Seibert could not be conclusively identified as the person who committed the egregious crimes. He tried to confuse the jury by discrediting the DNA analyst's work and asked the jury to consider hypothetical contamination that could have occurred at the crime lab.

He attempted to discredit the testimony of one of Seibert's ex-wives and his girlfriend, saying they just had axes to grind.

He was insistent that local law enforcement was in such a rush to appease the nervous residents of Miami that they randomly chose Seibert, an ordinary guy, as their sacrificial lamb.

At one point, the defense attorney likened the police investigation to "President George Bush's talks about weapons of mass destruction in Iraq."

The defense tried to cast doubt on the difference between Michael Seibert's actual appearance and the sketch produced by the forensic artist. They argued that I had described the eyes completely wrong for the sketch artist and that it couldn't have possibly been him.

In a final maddening attempt to sow doubt, the defense questioned my "performance" on the stand. He actually accused me of "hamming it up" in the witness box. The attorney reasoned that it had been four years since the rapes and that I shouldn't still be so emotional. "It's common sense," he declared. He told the jury that traumatic feelings resolve over time and that my tears were nothing more than theatrics. He even repeated an old adage his wife used to tell him, "Never underestimate an apparently helpless blond. Watch out!"

He went further, arguing that I may have completely imagined the violence, including the presence of a knife, to justify the extreme sexual acts I participated in that day. Basically, the core argument was that it was not his client and that I was a drama queen with a bad memory and an agenda. I was a woman so hell-bent on having someone pay for what allegedly happened to me that I was willing to accuse an innocent man.

Moments later, after delivering his speech full of personal attacks, he demanded the jury find his client not guilty and took his seat. I felt like I had been raped all over again. The trial may have been ending, but my body was still absorbing the violence of his words.

For a moment, before they released the jury for deliberations, I escaped into a quiet place inside my mind to rest. It was over. I had done all that I could do, and now a random group of strangers would decide my rapist's fate. It was no longer my responsibility. When the jury left the room, the silence shattered into movement.

I remember stepping out into the area outside of the courtroom where everyone from the public gallery was milling around like ants on a hill. I stuck close to my family while we waited for the verdict. I avoided eye contact with people, trying to engage only with my court-appointed advocates. I quickly became overwhelmed by the scene, and with every passing minute, my anxiety grew.

I wondered what was taking so long, although we had only been waiting for about an hour. Did they not think he was guilty? Was the jury fooled by his clean-cut appearance and normal family upbringing? In my mind, it was an open and shut case, but maybe they didn't see it that way. I hadn't let myself imagine what my world would be like if he were acquitted, but now those suffocating thoughts were creeping in. That was when I noticed them.

At one point, I spotted Michael Seibert's family standing just down the hall from us. They were cloistered together, just like my family was. They seemed to be encouraging each other, smiling as they chatted. I am sure they were nervous too, countering every prayer for justice that I sent up to heaven with a few of their own.

When I sensed their eyes looking my way, I glanced up. I made brief eye contact with his parents and immediately knew that in their hearts, it was me who was the enemy. As much as I wanted to, I couldn't begrudge them for that. The love a parent has for a child is designed to be irrationally unconditional. I stepped into a side room to catch my breath, shaken to my core by the importance of what was about to happen. Time stretched and collapsed all at once.

After about two and a half hours, the judge summoned everyone back inside the courtroom. I would later learn that the verdict came relatively fast, given the severity of the charges. With my palms sweating and heart racing, I took my seat. I held onto Jamie's hand as if my life depended on it. It seemed like everything was moving in slow motion as the judgment was read. I don't remember all of the discussions from the bench, but I do remember hearing the only word that mattered to me … eight times in succession.

Guilty.

Guilty.

Guilty.

Guilty.

Guilty.

Guilty.

Guilty.

Guilty.

20

When Justice Found Its Voice

JUSTICE HAD BEEN DECIDED, but it was not yet complete. A conviction determines guilt; sentencing determines consequence. Between the two, there is a pause—a strange, suspended space where relief and dread coexist. My body felt electrified, and my soul finally felt free to shout in the sheer joy of justice. We were safe. Our suffering was validated. Evil was held accountable. Happy tears flowed from my eyes. The celebration was brief. Unfortunately, the waiting was not.

Five long weeks passed between the conviction and the sentencing. The court needed time to do a presentencing investigation of the defendant's background and circumstances so that the judge could render a fair and appropriate sentence. They looked into Seibert's childhood, education, work history, mental health status, financial situation, and other factors that might be viewed as mitigating.

During this time, I had my own assignment keeping me busy: the victim impact statement. It was supposed to be directed at the judge, but since Seibert would be present in court, it was a way for me to address him and let him know the damage he had done. I wanted to make it perfect. It would be the most vulnerable and desperate speech I would ever give, but at the same time, hopefully the most empowering. When the day finally came, the weight of it settled into my bones.

On December 15, 2006, my family and I walked into the courthouse for the final time. Seibert and his family were there too. He was not in a suit this time, but rather shackled in an orange jumpsuit. I felt safer now than I did during the trial, which made it slightly easier to be brave.

When the judge asked if I would like to make a statement, I summoned all of the strength I had saved up for this very moment and began to speak. My voice was soft at first, but gradually grew louder. What follows is my victim impact statement, read aloud to the court on December 15, 2006.

Dear Judge Adrien:

> Writing an impact statement for a crime like that one that I was a victim of is certainly a daunting task. How does one briefly summarize all of the devastating effects kidnapping and rape have on one's life? Even more tragic to explain are the effects those acts have on one's children. I will do my best to explain what my family has been through and, in doing so, hopefully explain why I believe that Michael Seibert deserves the maximum sentence allowed for each of his eight convictions.
>
> The morning of October 16, 2002, started out like any other day for my family. My daughter went off happily to school, my husband to work, and my son and I spent time doing errands. That was to be the last normal morning of our lives. From the moment Michael Seibert hit me over the head and kidnapped my family, nothing would ever be the same for any of us. The time that he spent threatening

us, hurting us, and robbing us has forever clouded the way we view the world. Neighborhoods no longer look safe, and strangers look like potential attackers.

For me, the trauma of the rape has impacted every single day of my life since it happened. Even now, over four years later, I seldom go for more than a few minutes without some image or feeling from the rape popping into my mind. Whether it is the image of my rapist's face or the sound of my screaming children or the feeling of complete helplessness as he drove us into the middle of nowhere, I am a constant prisoner of my thoughts. I suffer from both an anxiety disorder and clinical depression as a result of what has happened to me. I am unable to sleep and, when sleep does come, it is often interrupted by horrifying nightmares. Sometimes I feel like I will never be normal again.

Although my children were not heard from at the trial, Michael Seibert's conviction is about what he did to each of them that day as well. My daughter Mia was only three when this terrible event happened. She lost her innocence that day in my van when she was physically hurt by Michael Seibert, trying to escape abduction and, most importantly, when she was forced to watch every minute of the brutal rape and beating of her mother. Michael Seibert repeatedly threatened to kill Mia with a knife and to drown our family by sinking our van into the canal near where he parked.

Although my daughter is a smart, beautiful little girl, she carries deep within her a constant reminder of how dark and terrifying the world can be. Mia experiences nightmares and other sleep problems. She has seen multiple therapists who specialize in trauma counseling and in treating victims of childhood sexual violence. She also suffered some behavioral regression as a result of her kidnapping, including the fact that she did not give up diapers completely or use the bathroom at preschool normally until after she was 4 years old.

My son was also traumatized that day. He was an eight-month-old infant who was forced to scream and cry for three hours without any comfort from his mother, who was being raped right before his eyes. My son was wet and hungry and scared … too little to understand why his mommy wasn't helping him.

The real problems for my son started after the rape when I stopped being able to mother him properly. I was too emotionally wrecked and traumatized to pay attention to everything he needed. More importantly, I was unable to even look at him for weeks because my rapist made sure I looked into Peter's eyes during the most intense parts of the rape. After the attack, every time I looked at my son, I remembered with crystal clear detail how it felt to be raped by Mr. Seibert. After the rape and abduction, the impacts on our lives could be felt in other ways as well.

For my husband, he was unable to concentrate at work. He was always worried about our safety and suffering from his own bout with post-traumatic stress disorder. Our whole family dynamic changed after the rape, with him having to take on more responsibilities at home while I fought to return to normal.

Because Michael Seibert was on the run for over five months after the rape, we lived in constant fear that he would come back to kill me and my children. After all, he knew where we lived, knew where we went to church, and had threatened to come back for us and finish us off if I ever told anyone.

I stayed locked in my house and never went anywhere alone. I had my mom come sit with my son and me every day until my husband got home from work, and I had friends do errands for me and take my daughter to school. I was a prisoner in my own house.

My family and other caregivers were exhausted. At one point, to give my mom a break, I even hired someone to stay with me during the days to protect me and watch Peter, so I could try to get some sleep. It finally became too much to bear, and we made the painful decision to leave Miami.

The decision to leave was very difficult on all of us. I grew up in Miami and had my parents less than two miles away—a nice perk when you have two small children and are as emotionally close as my family is. My husband had a good job with an engineering firm where he had been for over six years. We loved our home and our neighborhood and planned on living in Miami forever.

Unfortunately, the rape and kidnapping put our security in jeopardy and replaced our good feelings about our neighborhood with frightening memories. We had no other choice; my husband quit his job, and we put our house up for sale. We left Miami behind. Although our new community has provided us with a fresh start, we will always miss Miami and are sad we had to leave for such terrible reasons.

I could go on forever about the impact Michael Seibert's actions have had on the lives of every person in my family. He changed our whole world. He took away our notion of security, drove us from a life we loved, left us with emotional scars bigger than you can imagine, and has made us his prisoners for life.

I will never stop living in the shadow of what he has done. He forever changed the path for all of us and will always occupy a corner in my mind. I will never, ever be truly free! He broke my dreams and destroyed the life I wanted for my family. For that, forgiveness may never come.

During the time Michael Seibert held us hostage, he did his best to shake my faith in God. Throughout the entire ordeal, he questioned my beliefs and spouted hateful things about religion and the church. He took an act as despicable as rape and tried to use that act to defile my God as well.

Today, I want to say out loud, in my attacker's presence, that one of the only positive things about this rape is that it has made my faith even stronger. I know God did not abandon me even for a second on that hot October day. He was right beside me through it all, and I know that He will someday, in His time, find a way to bring something good from this situation. I will never lose faith.

And likewise, as determined as Michael Seibert was to destroy "women like me … innocent women with families … women he felt needed to pay for his miserable existence," he failed there as well. I am, deep down too strong for that. And no matter what, my family will never fail to stick together.

> Like Ernest Hemingway once wrote, I feel that eventually this rape will make us all "stronger in the broken places."
>
> In the end, I ask that Michael Seibert's reckless and violent disregard for the lives of my family be taken very seriously and that he is given all seven life sentences he is eligible to receive. He needs to pay for all three lives he kidnapped and threatened to take that day, and for the beatings he gave me, and for the money he stole from us.
>
> He needs to pay separately for each of the four times he raped me with a deadly weapon in front of my children and made me believe in my heart that I would die if I didn't comply with his every demand. He took away our lives that day in October 2002, and I plead with the court to take away his freedom forever in return."

When I finished reading, the courtroom was silent. I looked my rapist in the eye one last time before I sat back down and saw nothing but emptiness and evil. There was immense satisfaction in being able to give my statement and prove to the man who tried to destroy me that hot October day that he had failed. I was stronger. My God was stronger. We had won.

My mom, dad, and husband all gave statements at the sentencing too. Hearing my parents describe their anguish, at times through tears, was gut-wrenching. I hated listening to their pain. I am so grateful, however, that they were given the opportunity to tell the judge what was in their hearts. Michael Seibert's actions forever changed their lives too.

Jamie definitely had not planned to speak in court that day. My husband is an engineer, a math guy. He is also a bit of an introvert, so public speaking and sharing his emotions in front of strangers are not easy feats for him. I was shocked to my core when he stood up and spontaneously began talking. It was like he had been overtaken by a supernatural force and couldn't keep his rage inside anymore.

His message was short but powerful. Jamie told the judge that our family had been to hell and back, but would remain together forever because we love each other. In addition to that love, we have respect for the people in our lives. It was then, while speaking about respect, that my husband looked at Michael Seibert in the eye and began his elegant oratory.

He declared that there was no way that Seibert loved or respected anyone or anything. No decent father would disrespect his own kids by committing such grotesque crimes against a mother and her children. He went on to say that Seibert did not respect his own parents, one a church volunteer and one a retired federal law enforcement agent, who had presumably tried to raise him to be a kind person.

Jamie finished by saying that Seibert definitely doesn't have the ability to respect the rule of law and must never be allowed out to hurt us or anyone else ever again. I was so proud of my husband for doing what he must have feared the most, confronting the man who almost killed his family.

Then it was the defense's turn to speak. The defendant's family was also given the opportunity to speak to the judge about the effect the crimes had on them and to humanize their son. Seibert's father stood and delivered his statement; his voice was strong but tinged with anguish. While it was nauseating to listen to anyone defend the man who wanted to kill me, I could understand his father's desperation.

He said that no one in their family believed that Michael could have committed any of the horrendous crimes he was charged with. Since Michael's birth forty-five years prior, they had not witnessed any behavior at all that indicated he could possibly be guilty of this level of depravity. It just couldn't be true.

The most impactful part of his statement was when he talked about the phone call he got from law enforcement, informing him that they were looking for his son and the nature of the charges against him. "I cried like a baby. If I had been told that my son had murdered someone, robbed someone, I would have accepted that more easily than I could this evil offense."

I sat in shock that even Seibert's own father could appreciate the gravity of rape. He closed by saying he wished that the system could determine exactly what happened that day, but that it never would. He summarized the case against his son by saying that we are all left to wonder, forever, who committed this crime and why it happened. The little bit of empathy I had faded in that moment. Was he calling me a liar? We all knew for certain that his son was the perpetrator.

He went on to say that his family believed in the presence of evil in the world and its power to overtake lives. Seibert's father was grateful for Michael's love for God, saying that over the last few years, they had discussed the Bible and prayed together during calls from the prison. I was stunned. It was hard for me to reconcile what he was saying with my own personal experiences with his son—a man who repeatedly blasphemed God while raping me; a man who tried to scare my daughter by saying that God had abandoned us and hated us.

After reaffirming his unconditional love for his child, he spoke the most jarring words I had heard yet: "Your honor, my wife and

I both believe this: We would rather have Michael here in prison accepting the Lord than out on the streets as an atheist." His words were like a knife in my heart at first, but then they offered a sweet release. As a parent and a Christian myself, I understood the magnitude of what his father was saying. For a brief second, I even felt a disturbing wave of heaviness come over me, being the person who demanded Seibert's incarceration for life.

As a victim of a life-altering crime, however, I immediately tried to give myself some grace for feeling like his father put far too positive a spin on his son's impending sentence. In my grief, I truly felt like there should be no "bright side" to any of this. As I anxiously awaited the sentence, I experienced a freeing revelation.

What happened in Seibert's life moving forward was not up to me. The facts of the case clearly mandated that he be punished severely for his actions. What happened to the man in eternity, however, would be handled between him and God. I was out of the equation. I had done everything that was mine to do to get earthly justice for my family. Heavenly justice was not my responsibility, and that was a relief.

Unfortunately, my momentary peace was interrupted by the surprising revelation that Michael Seibert asked to make his own statement to the judge. He chose silence during the trial, but now I would have to hear his voice. I wasn't mentally prepared to listen to him proclaim his innocence and ask for leniency, but he did. His words burned like fire in my ears.

He began his plea to the court by referring to the points my husband made in his victim impact statement about respect. I took a special joy in knowing that he had been listening and that Jamie's words had especially gotten under his skin. Seibert said he had always treated everyone he encountered with the utmost respect, including his children, his parents, and his faith. He boldly declared, "I'm not a person to hold children hostage and attempt to kill them. That's not me."

My mouth fell open when he summed up the crime with that powerful description of what actually happened in the van. I wanted to scream, *You did hold them hostage, and you wanted to kill them. Beautifully said, Michael.* Seibert repeatedly stated his innocence and blamed everyone else for his situation. When asked about the DNA evidence directly linking him to the crime, he said that if he had to get into that, "we would be here forever," trying to cast doubt on the validity of the analysis. He used his upbringing as proof that he couldn't be the man who committed these atrocities, and even went so far as to boast about what a great father he was.

He offered up the example of how he occasionally used his lunch hour to volunteer as a reader in his son's kindergarten class. He claimed ineffectiveness of counsel and blamed his attorney for not presenting an expert forensic scientist as a witness who would have successfully contradicted the prosecution's DNA claims. He insisted that he was an innocent victim.

After the prosecution and defense made their final summations, the judge was quick to pronounce the sentence. He addressed the courtroom with a somber tone and stated that Michael Seibert's crimes undisputedly destroyed several families. In response to the defense attorney's request to temper the sentence because no one was killed or disfigured, the judge asserted that rape is an especially devastating form of mental disfigurement.

This event would live in my mind and echo in the lives of my children forever. The damage to each of us was permanent and irreparable. The judge agreed with the State Attorney's argument that each rape represented a separate event and must be treated individually. He also acknowledged the real threat that Michael Seibert posed to the community if he were someday released, speaking to his pathological obsession with violence against women.

The day ended with our perpetrator receiving a sentence that exceeded any punishment I had dared to hope for. I had prepared myself for the worst, knowing that courts often do not always maximize penalties for people who commit acts of a sexual nature.

I was hoping in my heart to accomplish the goal I set when I rejected the original 30-year plea deal: to keep him locked up until he died. That result would make the extra years we spent navigating the heartbreaks of the criminal justice system worth it in the end. The gamble paid off handsomely.

Michael Seibert received a separate life sentence for each of the people he kidnapped on October 16, 2002, and a separate one for every time he raped me at knifepoint. He got a total of SEVEN life sentences, plus fifteen years for the robbery, to be served consecutively. It was both a concrete victory and a semantic one. The judge's ruling locked him up for the rest of his natural life while conceptually acknowledging that each event mattered enough to take away his freedom for multiple lifetimes.

People in the courtroom, including myself, audibly gasped at the result. Then came the smiles, hugs, and happy tears. Sweet, overwhelming justice had been served. He would lose his freedom and his power forever. I watched as Seibert shuffled out of the courtroom in chains. That was the last time I would ever have to see him in person—no more looking over my shoulder.

I exited the courthouse with my family as they shielded me from the swarms of media waiting outside. Jamie and I spent that night at my parents' house, absorbing the victory. The next morning, we drove home to see our kids.

It felt strange to have the trial and sentencing behind us. The crime and subsequent involvement with law enforcement and the judicial system had been a part of our lives every single day for over four years. We didn't know what the future would hold, but it was time to turn the page and start a new chapter.

21

What Closure Really Means

FORTUNATELY, CHRISTMAS WAS JUST ten days after the sentencing. It was a blessed distraction. I filled my time trying to be fully present and full of holiday spirit for my kids, who were now seven and almost five years old. The previous four Christmases were tainted by my deep depression and the ongoing quest for justice. There were very few Norman Rockwell-like memories to recall.

This year, however, it felt good to finally revel in festive feelings of the season. New Year's Day was filled with resolutions to repair the damage of the past and to reset our capacity to feel joy again. Nightmares and flashbacks were still happening, but at least I could banish them to the quiet nighttime hours and enjoy family time out in the open without crippling fear. With the trial behind us and the noise finally quieted, I found myself confronting a different kind of reckoning—one that had nothing to do with courtrooms or verdicts.

Before I continue on, I want to take this moment to say a few words about closure. After I declined the plea deal in my case, many people outside of my family criticized my decision to press on to trial. They kept using the word "closure." Closure is a myth, they claimed, and a conviction would not heal the hurt in my heart or give me my old life back. They reasoned that my decision to go to trial would only serve to drag out the pain and negatively affect the mental health of my husband and kids. Trying to achieve closure after a crime like mine was, in their judgment, an impossible and selfish goal.

I listened to what they said and beat myself up some days, trying to force myself to believe them. But my heart just couldn't buy into the idea. It occurred to me that some people on the outside, and maybe a few on the inside, might have just wanted the crime-and-punishment phase of the event to be over because they themselves were uncomfortable still having to hear about it.

That realization forced me to step back and examine what closure actually means—and who gets to define it.

What constitutes closure is unique among individuals. This is especially true for victims of violent crimes, since nobody experiences the effects of trauma in the same way, even if their experiences are similar. I knew this from my own situation. Multiple women had their lives affected by Michael Seibert, and each one had a different journey, or individual lens, through which to evaluate their own notion of justice and cope with life after rape.

Not everyone finds closure through traditional avenues or definitions, and I stand firm in my belief that every person should be given the opportunity to pursue what justice looks like for them without judgment. What's of paramount importance is that every survivor is given options—and the opportunity to control how his or her story will end.

Closure for me was never going to be defined as reaching the end of the journey, thereby closing the book on the event and its influence over my life. Rather, I think I saw the opportunity to get closure as a chapter in my life story that would ultimately be a component of my ongoing healing. I would use it to shore up a new foundation and rebuild my life.

For me, the process I went through with the trial and the sentencing absolutely provided that for me. I got to use my voice to hold a violent criminal justly accountable, take away his freedom here on earth, and conclusively end my fear that he would be able to hurt my family or others again.

Ending that chapter gave me the ability to free myself and to use closure as a building block on which to reframe and reimagine my life. I could take my story in a new direction now. It might be different than the one I set out to write as a child, but equally beautiful and fulfilling if I kept authoring it with hope.

What I didn't yet understand was that my closure was not an ending—it was an opening. With the fear that had governed my life finally quieted, something else began to stir in its place. I was no longer fighting to survive or to be believed. For the first time in years, I had room to ask a different question: What now? The answer would come slowly, and unexpectedly, but it would lead me beyond healing and into purpose.

22

The Birth of Advocacy

IN THE MONTHS AFTER the trial, I tried to stop thinking about crime and pivot toward other interests. I had to find something to do with my extra time and energy. At the beginning of 2007, I got more involved at the kids' school and even agreed to be an officer for the PTO the following school year. I was excited to channel all of the fight I found within myself during the trial into leadership and volunteerism. I truly loved every moment. I ended up being on the PTO Board for four years, serving with fantastic women who are still some of my closest friends today.

My kids could see me thriving in this new role. I wanted, more than anything, to help them regain a sense of security in the world, and this opportunity allowed me to do fulfilling work while maintaining a steady presence in their everyday routines. Both kids exhibited some symptoms of PTSD during this time, and I wanted to be able to advocate or comfort them when needed.

For a quick minute, I had entertained going back to my "prechild" career, but I made peace with myself when I realized I needed the flexibility of volunteerism. I was a wholly different person now, and needed some time to figure out my place in the world as a woman and a parent. For a brief season, it felt like I had found my footing again—like justice had given me permission to breathe and begin rebuilding a quieter, safer life. But that sense of calm would not last.

Simultaneously, while I was figuring out my new path in 2007, a series of criminal events was unfolding in a suburb just 45 minutes south of where we lived. In hindsight, these crimes became the original catalyst for my life of advocacy. It was not anything I could have predicted, but the frightening events that were happening gave me a reason to ultimately resurrect my voice.

Reality hit me hard, and the media coverage of the crimes shook me out of the temporary bliss that I had been in, feeling safe and untouchable since my perpetrator had been sentenced to life behind bars. I came to the unfortunate conclusion that evil is not isolated. Rather, it is present everywhere, and my family, as a result, was probably not immune to experiencing it again.

The details were different, but the pattern felt hauntingly familiar—and that recognition unsettled me more than I wanted to admit.

In March of 2007, just four months after the sentencing in my case, a woman was abducted in Boca Raton, Florida, from the Boca Town Center Mall's parking lot and killed. Her body was discarded in a local park hours after being shot to death. Five months later, in August 2007, a mother and her two-year-old son were abducted from the parking lot of the same mall. They were taken to a nearby ATM and forced to withdraw money, after which the assailant tied them up and returned them to the shopping center before fleeing. In December 2007, another mother and her seven-year-old daughter were also carjacked from the Boca Town Center and taken to an ATM to withdraw cash. Tragically, both mother and child were later found dead in their car in the parking lot, bound and shot in the head.

Police believed that the cases were the work of a single predator, given that they had similar modus operandi. The crimes all involved daytime stranger abductions, robberies from ATMs, the victims' cars being returned to the mall, and, in two instances, involved the presence of young children. It all struck too close to home. I felt helpless. There were more psychopaths out there using a similar, perverted playbook for their crimes. I was overwhelmed with fear again. I couldn't unsee the parallels. To calm myself, I decided to seek help in the pages of a book that had been gifted to me in the weeks after my assault.

The mother of one of my college roommates sent me the memoir of Patricia Weaver Franciso called *Telling*. In the book, the author recounts her own sexual assault, her fifteen-year trudge towards justice and healing, and the life lessons that stemmed from it all. One of my favorite parts of the book is when she writes, "Remaining in the role of the victim is dangerous, though.... The people most able to change the world are those motivated by inside knowledge. You who see, tell the others."

It awakened something inside of me, a sense of responsibility, to go make the world better for victims who were struggling to be heard or validated. In the idea that I was in possession of unique knowledge about what rape and its aftermath felt like, I found my call to action. I could use my voice not only to explain the long-ranging effects of evil, but I could also try to prevent it from happening to someone else. For the first time since the trial ended, I felt the familiar tightening in my chest that signaled purpose, not fear, returning.

At the start of 2008, with the Boca Town Center murders still unsolved, I set out on a mission to publicly share my own personal safety tips with women in the county. I truly believed that these simple tips might have prevented me from becoming a crime victim or at least might have given me a fighting chance to get away.

This list of tips used my rapist's own confessed strategies for hunting unsuspecting mothers. It became a template of what not to do. Being privy to Seibert's thought process with regard to what makes someone a "perfect target," I created flyers filled with recommendations for moms to use to limit their vulnerability.

I started passing them out at our church's preschool in Jupiter. That evolved into me speaking at my church's Mothers of Preschoolers (MOPS) group and eventually being asked to present at other community preschools and MOPS groups in the area.

The local CBS station caught wind of what I was doing from an anonymous Palm Beach County mom who felt my story was worth sharing with viewers. They did a short interview with me, and I suddenly found myself quite busy promoting a grassroots safety campaign across the area out of my car. What began as a quiet attempt to regain control of my own fear was quickly becoming something larger than me.

The groups I volunteered to speak to were all appreciative of my time and candor about what I experienced. Many women I spoke to said they never imagined that evil could lurk in safe spaces like church parking lots and that the presentations made them more vigilant.

A few discussed their own rapes with me privately, assaults that they had never confessed to anyone else out of fear of not being believed or supported. Some never told anyone because they blamed themselves for allowing the assaults to happen. The women I spoke with carried loads of unresolved trauma inside of them, and I tried to explain to them that the weight of this shame was never theirs to carry.

This became a recurring theme after my presentations, and I found myself wanting to do more for the women who confided in me. I volunteered to connect the women I met with state and local resources, as well as toll-free 24-hour national hotlines like the one provided by the Rape Abuse and Incest National Network (RAINN). I had personally turned to RAINN's hotline after we moved to Palm Beach County when I didn't know where to go for help.

During this time, I wrote an email to RAINN and thanked them for their organization's commitment to supporting survivors. Some of the advice that they passed down to me in my darkest hours inspired me to keep fighting for justice and not to give up hope. It definitely made me feel less alone.

I applied to the speaker's bureau listed on their website and let them know about my one-woman show, spreading safety tips to women's groups. It felt good to connect with this large organization that was doing important work for rape survivors at the national level. I wasn't confident my message would actually reach anyone who really cared about my project, which I began calling "Keeping Moms Safe," but it was satisfying to know that my desire to make a difference had been sent out into the universe.

Just as I was beginning to believe that this chapter of advocacy might finally stand on its own, the past found a way to intrude once again. During this time, I found myself on the phone again with the State Attorney's office, this time facing another type of legal fight—the appellate process. I had truly hoped my chapter with Michael Seibert was over. Unfortunately, it seems that I was naïve to think he would just slink away and serve his punishment.

Postcards from the State Attorney's office routinely arrived in my mailbox with status updates. I was on edge again, scared he would win his appeal and that we would go back to square one. Seibert argued the ineffectiveness of counsel, the trial venue, and anything else he could come up with. It was both retraumatizing and frustrating.

I was at the point in my journey where I didn't want to be an active participant in the criminal justice process anymore. Life now was about healing and moving forward with my plans to help others and bring something good out of what had happened.

I resented the intrusion.

I had my closure.

23

The Cost of Survival

I KEPT MYSELF CONSTANTLY busy so that I didn't have time to think about the chance that we might have to go back to court. My attorney, Laura Adams, returned to her role as my rock and legal angel anytime things got messy again. Before I was victimized by crime, I watched the news just like anyone else. I would be outraged by the stories of violence, but would naturally forget about the victims once some time had passed. Now, I knew firsthand how much survivors still need support in the aftermath.

We can't just abandon survivors when a crime is over, or a trial is finished. For most survivors, there are a multitude of triggering reminders of their trauma that resurface over time. With good care, survivors can heal and learn to coexist with the pain, but we as a community must never minimize it. That understanding didn't come from theory or research; it came from watching trauma continue to unfold inside my own home.

On the home front, Jamie and I tried our hardest as parents to provide as much stability for our children as we could. Jamie worked insanely long hours at his office, sometimes until midnight, so that he could be involved in their activities. He coached the kids' soccer teams, lacrosse teams, and was actively involved with Cub Scouts. I was at the elementary school almost daily, as a PTO board member, room mother, and classroom volunteer.

There was a drive inside both of us to make up for the years of sadness and uncertainty that our children had witnessed. Neither of us will ever regret one moment we spent on the field or at their schools. It helped heal us too. For a time, that immersion in ordinary life felt like protection, like our love and presence could help them outrun the past.

The elementary school years were especially precious and allowed us relatively unfettered access into our children's worlds as they were finding their way. We knew their friends, had some control over what they were exposed to, and could quickly step in to guide and protect them. All of that inevitably started to change, however, when they advanced into the upper grades.

As they moved through adolescent milestones, we quickly learned that kids store trauma in very complex ways. Despite all of our efforts, we would soon see the true impact that early childhood exposure to violence can have on a person. By the time middle school arrived, that delayed understanding collided with emotional volatility.

In children who have experienced violence, basic human growth and development can bring with it harsh realizations. Previously incomprehensible events in the world start to come into context just as these kids start to develop their own sense of identity, safety, and attachment. Unfortunately, when they can finally start putting the horrific pieces together and understand what happened in their past, they have already replayed the confusing and painful events in their minds to a very damaging level. Processing things like crime and mortality can be extremely retraumatizing at this stage. It is a fresh wound without the balm of innocence.

Navigating the middle school years is rough for almost everyone. Fluctuating hormones and friendships, coupled with a shaky sense of independence, can be quite destabilizing. Studies have shown that when adolescents who have experienced childhood trauma reach this stage in life, typical stressors can cause exceptionally disabling levels of distress. Sleep issues, depression, and chronic anxiety in these cases are practically universal.

As a parent, you pray that the world will be kind and not add to your child's pain while you try your best to build them up. Unfortunately, it doesn't always work out that way, and their pain becomes compounded.

One of the first manifestations of PTSD in adolescents is difficulty trusting others. My daughter, who, up until middle school, focused on gymnastics, books, and friends, never spoke about what happened to us with anyone outside of the family or medical community. Even then, she was very tight-lipped. She still is. When she finally did confide in someone close to her, they broke her trust. Gossip in the sixth grade tends to spread like wildfire.

Her story was passed around carelessly like an old-fashioned game of telephone, and the sense of security that we had spent years rebuilding with her was once again destroyed. The psychological wounds of abandonment and betrayal are some of the worst collateral damage that spawned out of the original crime. Watching how it all played out forced me to reconsider the way I had compartmentalized my own advocacy.

Prior to the "outing" of the story, my kids weren't really aware of all of the grassroots work I did in the county. I kept it mostly hidden, confined to school hours so that I wouldn't have to worry about their friends finding out. I never talked about what I did openly at home out of fear that they would mistakenly internalize it as a sign that I wasn't healing or that where we lived was unsafe.

However, now that my daughter, and then consequently my son, were experiencing the harsh lessons of other people's insensitivity and their own bouts with PTSD, I realized I needed to show them that our story could make a positive difference in the lives of others and even perhaps make the world a safer place.

My motivation for the mission became more powerful when I devoted myself to making them proud, rather than ashamed, of what we had endured. In that moment, advocacy stopped being something I did quietly for strangers and became something I modeled intentionally for my children.

Faith became the lens through which I reframed both our suffering and our responsibility. Living out the Bible verse Romans 8:28—a message of hope and assurance that, even in difficult times, God is in control and is working all things for the good. Like the mother I was that tragic day in the van, I resolved to fight in honor of them in everything I did going forward. I became determined to prove to them, and to others, that beautiful things can still come out of life's worst situations.

I reaffirmed the promise I made to God as my rapist pressed the tip of his knife into my neck—a promise to walk through every door He opened for me if we survived. I vowed to do my best to be a warrior for change in the world. That would be our family's legacy, and hopefully something they could be proud of in the future. That resolve pushed me beyond personal advocacy and into spreading systemic awareness.

During my own personal healing, I spent a great deal of time on sexual assault awareness websites. Earlier on in my budding advocacy, I learned that less than 3 percent of rapists ever spend a day in jail. That statistic meant that 97 percent of these sexual predators were free to roam the streets and potentially offend again. My mind was blown, and I felt an even greater sense of urgency to help turn the tide. Those numbers were unacceptable, and the system needed to be fixed.

I hoped to figure out how to improve the reporting rate of rape in Palm Beach County and spread the word about the services currently available to the community. In researching what agencies assisted local crime victims, I came across information about Palm Beach County's Victims' Rights Coalition. Although I was not an agency, but rather a lone survivor, I showed up at their next meeting.

I was blessed to meet a group of wonderful people who had been dedicated to serving crime victims for years. They appreciated my perspective and allowed me to stay as a "survivor representative." As I listened, it became clear that individual courage alone was not enough—systems mattered.

After attending months of meetings and events, I became bold and asked to have an informal lunch with several sex crimes prosecutors who worked for the county. During that meeting, I learned about breakdowns in the current system and the things they felt needed improvement. We collectively reasoned that if we could find a way to better serve victims from start to finish, the reported cases would have a better shot at a conviction.

After that meeting, I was introduced to several additional agencies and a few legislators, who were willing to help with the mission for change. To figure out the next steps, I turned inward and examined more closely why my rapist was part of that tiny 3 percent of offenders who are officially incarcerated. Why was our case different, and how did we find the strength to complete the grueling four-year road to justice?

The answer could be found in our experiences with the Miami-Dade County Sexual Assault Response Team (SART), which sprang into action as soon as I reported the crime. SART is a victim-centered, trauma-informed approach that an area can adopt to better serve both the immediate and long-term needs of victims of sexual violence. Fortunately for my family, Miami-Dade put together one of the first SARTs in the entire country long before we personally needed it.

A SART is multidisciplinary in nature, bringing together all of the professionals who will touch the life of a victim. It focuses on consistent, coordinated care and is designed to guide and support victims through the entirety of their involvement in the system. The core membership of a SART includes law enforcement, prosecutors, medical providers like forensic nurses, victim advocates, and crime lab analysts.

Linking all of these vital community actors together provides for better sharing of resources and the opportunity to troubleshoot challenges victims might face. Understanding this model fundamentally reshaped the way I viewed justice—not as a single verdict, but as a system capable of either supporting or abandoning survivors.

My own journey made me a huge supporter of this model of intervention. Outside research studies have also confirmed my belief that agencies that implement this type of framework produce a greater number of survivors reporting satisfaction with the criminal justice system. Sometimes, simply living and breathing after sexual assault can use up all of a survivor's strength.

I remember, especially in the immediate aftermath of the rapes, having a very finite amount of mental energy left over to figure out who I should be calling next to keep the process moving. A SART helps alleviate that anxiety by building a network of agencies that work hand-in-hand to proactively take care of a survivor and direct them towards the help they might not even know they need. Once I understood what was possible, it became impossible to ignore what was missing.

When I started to advocate for a more coordinated approach, Palm Beach County already had most of the actors necessary to build a SART. They had fantastic professionals who had been serving individuals for years in a more patchwork style of care. What my county lacked was coordinated protocols when it came to serving victims of sexual violence in a comprehensive way.

Victims of sexual violence deserve a system designed to gently transition them to the appropriate professionals during their healing and journey to justice. Knowing that the person you just entrusted your story to has a connection and full confidence in where you are going next relieves a lot of the anxiety inherent in the victim experience.

In Palm Beach County, however, there was still one major actor missing from the table before a successful SART could be created. I noticed its absence immediately upon moving to our new house back in 2003. Since the day of the assaults, I lived with the constant fear of being raped again, hovering in the back of my mind. I was in a new city now, where would I go if it happened? Where was the county's RCC?

I obviously grew troubled when I learned there was no certified rape crisis center in my new community, especially given the enormous size of the county. Where were rape victims taken? What happened to them? It seemed bizarre that a county with a population of over 1.3 million residents at the time had no need for a rape crisis center, especially when national crime statistics showed that one in six women in America was a victim of attempted or completed sexual assault in their lifetime.

With this in mind, it was inconceivable to me that any county in America could be without a center. I began thinking long and hard about how I could help bring an RCC to my new home.

24

When My Story Reached Capitol Hill

IN THE FALL OF 2010, I started to receive mass mailings from the RAINN Speakers Bureau that I had applied to months before. It felt nice to be included in a group of people who shared similar experiences and wanted to use their stories to affect change for others. Not long after the emails arrived, however, things began to change rapidly, and my mission and calling started to grow exponentially.

One unusually quiet morning, I received an unexpected call from Washington, DC. On the phone was a chipper legislative aide from Senator Arlen Spector's office (D-PA). As she and I talked, I couldn't stop pinching myself, trying to absorb everything she was saying.

I knew right from the start of the call who Senator Spector was. I always felt that he was one of the most interesting members of Congress. I followed his 30-year career in the news, from high school and college government classes all the way through to the present time, in part because my in-laws were his constituents.

At the time of the call, one of his many roles was Chairman of the Senate Judiciary Subcommittee on Crime and Drugs. The call served as an invitation from him to me to testify before the US Senate in a hearing to examine why rape is among the most underreported and underprosecuted crimes in America. His office, via RAINN, had heard about the legendary sentencing in my case and my personal efforts to help other victims through my grassroots safety campaign.

Senator Spector's office wanted me to share my full experience and what empowered me throughout my long journey to justice with other members of Congress. When I hung up, I just sat there for a moment, stunned—grateful, terrified, and keenly aware that saying yes would mean reopening the very story I had worked so hard to survive.

The opportunity to go to Capitol Hill and share my story was the fulfillment of a childhood dream. Since my time on the debate team, I had dreamed of using my speaking skills in public service one day as a congresswoman. Throughout college, I educated myself about the role and had unspoken fantasies of running for office one day.

Now here I was, a stay-at-home mom and "professional volunteer" from a tiny town in South Florida, getting a chance to speak on the big stage. The beauty of the moment was not lost on me as my heart swelled with gratitude. God had turned my tragedy into what felt like destiny.

Walking into the hearing room that day, I was struck by the weight of where I was. The wood-paneled walls, the long dais, the microphones and nameplates—all of it carried the quiet authority of decisions that ripple far beyond the room itself. This was no longer a courtroom or a community meeting. This was Capitol Hill, and the stakes felt much higher.

Flanked on either side by exhausted law enforcement officials and frustrated sexual assault victims with heartbreaking stories, I relished the opportunity to share with the senators how the "Miami Model" of victim-centered response saved my life. The evil my family experienced was both inconceivable and life-altering, but throughout our journey, we were always believed and never felt alone. Everyone involved with the case did their job correctly and followed the appropriate protocols.

We were sustained over the years leading up to the trial by professionals who prioritized victims, eventually turning the most vulnerable among us into strong survivors. Services like the ones we have are fortunate to have needed to be expanded throughout the nation and not just found in isolated pockets. The argument at the core of my testimony was that every American deserves the same standard of care and the opportunity to pursue their version of justice after a crime.

Sitting there, microphone in front of me, I understood something new: my story was no longer only about what had been done to me—it was about what was being done, or not done, for survivors everywhere. The room felt both formal and intimate at the same time—policy language layered over raw human pain.

It is incredible how a hearing like the one I was a part of can lead to meaningful, concrete change in a nation. As a result of this specific hearing, many important things were accomplished in our country. First, many states tackled the job of reforming their rape laws. This included expanding the definition of rape to encompass more than just vaginal-penile penetration, reducing the insistence on proof of resistance or severe injury, and excluding a victim's prior sexual history from court proceedings.

Next, the hearing highlighted the need for law enforcement to do a better job investigating allegations of rape and to devise effective training programs designed to improve victim involvement while eliminating gender bias. These programs must rely on better data collection about the scope of the problem and effective interventions.

Finally, the hearing introduced new concerns over the growing "rape kit backlog" across the US and demanded attention to this seldom-talked-about crisis. I didn't walk into that hearing expecting my life to expand. I walked into it expecting to tell the truth. But once I heard the scope of the problem, I couldn't unknow it.

For me, the hearing directly affected my life in two monumental ways. First, it gave me the opportunity to arrange a personal visit with my congressional representative at his office on Capitol Hill. I was able to directly express my concerns about Palm Beach County not having a certified RCC and what that meant overall for the welfare of survivors and community safety.

Second, it gave me an opportunity to learn about the horrifying and devastating reality of the nation's backlog of rape kits and provided me with a special invitation to get involved with federal legislative reform. Those two issues would consume all of my spare time for many years to come.

I left Washington with my head spinning—not from the grandeur of the place, but from the weight of what I now knew. I had walked in as a survivor with a story. I walked out as a woman with a mission.

25

The Hidden Backlog

BEFORE THE HEARING CHANGED the trajectory of my own advocacy, I was forced to confront a reality I had never known existed—one that would soon become central to my work and reshape my understanding of justice for survivors.

Prior to the hearing, organizations like RAINN were working with representatives on Capitol Hill to craft a bill to clear the existing backlog of nearly 400,000 sexual assault kits that were in storage across the country. It was intended to prevent this horrifying accumulation from ever happening again.

The issue was appalling to me. Why in the world were forensic evidence kits collecting dust on shelves instead of being analyzed at labs? Years prior, I watched the officer in my own case pick up my kit from the SANE before we left the RCC. It never even occurred to me that the envelope wouldn't be immediately submitted to the lab for testing. On TV and in the movies, evidence was handled with such urgency. Why was the reality so different for actual rape survivors in much of the country?

I once again counted my blessings that my assault happened in Miami, where there had been no sizable backlog, and my results were available relatively quickly. This was true for both my initial rape kit and the DNA recovered as a result of Seibert's fateful domestic violence arrest months later. My case was not an exception, but rather a product of the way Miami-Dade County Police and Crime Lab prioritized sexual assault kits within their system.

That realization, that my experience was shaped by policy and priorities rather than luck, would soon place me in an unexpected position. My positive experience with DNA testing at the crime lab unexpectedly qualified me to be a vocal advocate for survivors who had not received the same treatment. Just like with my Senate testimony, I was different from the other rape survivors who were called to advocate on the issue.

Their stories showed the heartbreaking realities of what happens when kits aren't tested, and justice is denied. They were painful lessons of what NOT to do. My story, however, served as a positive example of what was possible if states shifted their priorities in sexual assault kit testing, particularly through legislative change. It illustrated the importance of testing ALL rape kits in a timely manner to stop serial offenders and give survivors a better opportunity for justice and healing.

As I leaned into this role, I quickly learned that the problem was not simply logistical—it was deeply systemic. The more I learned about the reasons behind the backlog, the more passionate I became about driving change. I learned that in most jurisdictions, law enforcement personnel themselves decide whether to submit a rape kit for DNA testing. Reasons law enforcement may not submit a rape kit for testing can include constraints on funding, lab capacity, staffing, and equipment. More often, studies concluded that the major reason kits go unsubmitted may be law enforcement's negative perceptions of a sexual assault victim's credibility or sense of cooperation.

An investigation into the topic revealed that personal information about the victim's appearance, sobriety, relationship status, or the location and time of the crime heavily influenced the officers' judgment with respect to submitting a kit for testing. I never knew there was so much subjectivity surrounding such a crucial decision. Coming to terms with these failures clarified why legislative intervention was not optional—it was essential.

The federal bill I was asked to help advocate for would come during the 112th term of Congress. It was called the SAFER Act, which stood for the Sexual Assault Forensic Evidence Reporting Act. I started my advocacy shortly after my Senate testimony in late 2010 and immersed myself in learning everything I could about the process and the players. Fortunately, my prior education in government at the University of Virginia made me a quick study.

Basically, there are two sessions within a congressional term, each lasting one year, and I was active for the entirety of both. Over the two years I advocated on Capitol Hill, I witnessed several different iterations of the original bill and got rare insight into what actually drives cooperation and stymies policy in Washington, DC.

The experience was invaluable, completely changing many of my personal views on politics. I came to understand that advocacy was not a single moment of testimony—it was sustained, exhausting persistence.

From January 5, 2011, until January 3, 2013, I was constantly involved in getting the word out to congressional representatives and constituents about the backlog and the bill in every way possible. The first thing that needed to be done was to educate people about what the backlog actually was and to do it in a way that made them care about both rape survivors and community safety. I wrote emails, blasted information about the severity of the situation on my social media, and did countless TV interviews on the issue.

I flew to Washington, DC, and walked the halls of Capitol Hill many times, meeting directly with representatives and aides in the House and Senate. I told my story over and over again to anyone who would listen. It was exhausting to constantly talk about the worst day of my life, yet it was also extremely empowering.

The best part of my experience was seeing the softer side of politicians, especially the ones who seemed so stoic when the bright lights of the media were on them. Those quieter, unscripted moments reinforced why showing up in person mattered. Being able to connect with decision-makers face-to-face and share my personal journey, not as a paid lobbyist but simply as an individual survivor on a mission, was surreal. I felt like I was living out democracy in its purest form, experiencing the part of my childhood textbooks where they tell you that your voice can make a difference.

By this point, as a woman in my forties, I recognized that the very existence of the backlog was the result of decades of inherent bias and misconceptions in the system about what rape "is" and who constitutes a "true" victim. I knew from the work I was doing that hundreds of thousands of other rape victims in America had horrible experiences trying to get justice, many of them left feeling invalidated or invisible. As long as I could get lawmakers to listen, my goal was to use my singular voice to represent the collective group that felt silenced. That commitment carried me into dozens of difficult, but necessary, conversations.

Over the course of my visits to Washington, DC, to collect cosponsors for the SAFER Act, I met with supporters and skeptics in both political parties. Some could not wait to sign on as cosponsors of the bill, while others needed a fair bit of persuading. Some doubted that the legislation would offer any worthwhile change. It became my passion to show them that they were wrong.

I hoped they could see the intensity in my eyes while I spoke directly to them about the vital role DNA played in identifying my potentially deadly serial rapist. I hoped they could appreciate the freedom and security it restored to my family when we were able to experience closure through the justice system. What I wanted most was for them to find a call to action in the rawness of my words. I wanted them to tap into our shared humanity that demanded "Justice for All."

Every rape kit represents a person's suffering. Each kit collected is equally important. Lawmakers had the power to do something about the blatant injustice. The SAFER Act, however, did not emerge in a vacuum. This was not the first time representatives on Capitol Hill had heard about DNA as an indispensable tool to fight crime.

The Debbie Smith Act, passed in 2004, was the country's first piece of legislation that specifically targeted the DNA backlog. The SAFER Act was born out of that crucially important bill. It is named after a rape survivor, a woman who is now my friend, from Williamsburg, Virginia, who was brutally attacked in her home by an unknown assailant in 1989. Unfortunately, the DNA in Debbie's rape kit was not analyzed or uploaded into the FBI's database until 1994. In July of 1995, a match was definitively made and the perpetrator identified. He was already in jail when his identity was confirmed, serving time for the abduction and robbery of two other women.

He went to trial on Debbie's case in 1998 and received two life sentences plus twenty-five years for the crimes against her. I have had the distinct pleasure of meeting with Debbie and her husband, Rob, on several occasions and walking the halls of Congress with them. It has been an amazing experience to work with these two warriors who blazed the trail for DNA reform and continue to do so.

Standing on the shoulders of the Debbie Smith Act, the SAFER Act proposed additions to the existing law. It called for increased focus on recent DNA evidence from rape kits and addressed the backlog of untested rape kits, not only at labs but also those rape kits collecting dust in police storage around the country. This became known as the "hidden backlog," a concept most people were unfamiliar with.

The passage of the SAFER Act was of vital importance because it mandated that states applying for funds for testing kits were also required to audit and account for *all* kits that were collected and remained untested, so that they could get a more accurate picture of the problem. Passage of the SAFER Act required states to submit comprehensive plans to tackle their backlog and provide regular reports to the Department of Justice on their progress.

Funding would be increased for training for state and local agencies, capacity building, and faster analysis. The legislation was designed to provide greater transparency and efficiency in the criminal justice system, resulting in higher conviction rates and better outcomes for survivors.

As the 112th Congress neared its end in December 2012, the legislation looked like it was in a good position to pass as law in both the House and the Senate. I made one more trip to Washington, DC, just before Christmas, and was happy to see even the staunchest political foes agreeing on the importance of the act.

From my own state, Representative Debbie Wasserman Schultz, who was the chair of the Democratic National Committee, and Allen West, who was a leading member of the Republican-led Tea

Party Caucus, both ended up as cosponsors. This kind of bipartisan agreement was a remarkable feat and made me incredibly hopeful as the legislation approached the final vote after the holidays.

While the Senate's version of the SAFER Act passed unanimously on December 30, 2012, the House of Representatives' version could not be reconciled with it before the clock on the 112th Congress expired. Rather than the bill dying, however, its positive momentum continued into the 113th Congressional session.

Both the House and Senate versions quickly came into alignment at the start of the new Congress and, after receiving President Obama's signature in February 2013, the SAFER Act became law as Title X of the Violence Against Women Act (VAWA) Reauthorization. Rather than acting as a standalone bill, the SAFER Act was now included in VAWA, the landmark federal legislation passed over thirty years ago that fundamentally changed the way the United States recognizes and combats gender-based violence.

Reflecting now on how it all happened, I am in awe that we were able to get the legislation passed with unanimous support from all representatives and senators. I look on that day in American history with great pride.

When the legislative journey finally reached its end, the weight of what we had accomplished began to settle in. RAINN sent me an enormous bouquet of flowers the day after the SAFER Act finally passed. The card attached read "Julie, the SAFER Act is law because of you!" Of course, I knew that many other individuals and agencies fought hard for the legislation and that I was just one part of a larger group. The gesture, however, had an incredible effect on my spirit in the days and years that followed.

The words on the card validated something deep inside of me. They gave real purpose to what I had been doing for years, telling my story over and over again in the hope of creating lasting change for others. The passage of the SAFER Act was tangible proof that the pain my family went through was not in vain. It was concrete evidence that showed our tears were not wasted.

I still think about that card anytime I get tired and think my experience isn't worth repeating anymore. As uncomfortable as the story is, however, the change it helps create makes me want to keep talking for as long as it takes to eradicate sexual violence.

26

Building What Was Missing

WHILE MY WORK IN Washington focused on changing systems at the federal level, another outcome of my Senate testimony would take shape much closer to home, one that addressed a gap that policy alone could not fill.

After my first Senate testimony in October 2010, my life was forever changed in two ways. The first was that it launched my involvement in promoting DNA justice for sexual assault survivors. The second was far more personal. It gave me the opportunity to meet Congressman Ron Klein, my personal congressional representative, on Capitol Hill that day to discuss in person why Palm Beach County lacked a certified RCC.

As we chatted in his office, Representative Klein became concerned about our lack of an RCC and immediately connected me with the Director of Legislative Affairs for Palm Beach County, Todd Bonlarron. I shrieked at the sound of Todd's name. Of all the names I expected to hear that day, his was not one of them. At the time representative Klein offered to make the introduction, I had no idea how personally significant that phone call would be. It was just more proof that God's fingerprint was all over my story.

Todd and I grew up together and were close friends throughout childhood. We were both in Mr. Dilley's legendary fourth-grade class that I mentioned earlier, participated in Olympics of the Mind competitions, and he was even my date to the ninth-grade prom at the conclusion of junior high school. In high school, we were in many of the same classes and travelled together constantly on the oft-mentioned Miami-Palmetto debate team. We lived close to each other while growing up, and our families were also friends.

Life had taken us in different directions, but suddenly our paths intersected again for a reason far greater than nostalgia. I was, once again, blown away that someone from my little corner of suburban Miami had intersected with my new mission. The way it all played out was miraculous.

Once we realized that we were now living only about thirty minutes from each other in Palm Beach County, Todd and I immediately made plans to meet up at a local restaurant. It was so much fun to catch up on the past twenty years and realize that time had not changed our friendship at all. Todd brought along his assistant, Melissa McKinlay, and she joined in all of the laughs. She also listened intently to my story.

Todd and Melissa were both compassionate about the struggles sexual assault survivors go through and were enthusiastic about the idea of creating positive change in the community. They each had numerous connections in state and local government and reached out to find legislative sponsors for the project. The wheels were set in motion.

What began as a conversation between former classmates quickly expanded into something far bigger than any of us had anticipated. An enthusiastic team of county officials, law enforcement, the crime lab, and existing victim service providers came together quickly and helped push the project along at a rapid pace. State Senator Lizbeth Benacquisto, who lived in Palm Beach County at the time, fully supported the center's creation and used her strong voice from the beginning to advocate for funding from the Capitol in Tallahassee.

I think part of the reason the project ended up being so successful was that the people involved in the process knew in their hearts that it was the right thing to do. It was a passion project for many people who became personally invested in the mission as a result of their own harrowing experience with sexual assault, both spoken and unspoken.

For me, it was a dream come true. Another tangible example of how my family's pain could be turned into progress and help others. Proof that continues to grow more significant with every passing year. When the center was finally completed, we turned our attention to what it would represent, not just what it would provide.

By late fall 2011, the center was completed. It was aptly named the Butterfly House. The name felt like a perfect metaphor for what we were trying to accomplish in this sacred space. It conjured up the imagery of a caterpillar's journey into a cocoon of uncertainty and its eventual reemergence as a new creature full of strength and hope for the future. The butterfly, we hoped, would be a positive image for survivors that illustrates how extreme beauty can emerge from the darkest of experiences.

I personally experienced this powerful transformation during my journey at the Roxy Bolton Rape Crisis Center in Miami as a beneficiary of their nursing and SART services. Like so many trauma survivors before me, I gained newfound strength, wisdom, and a deeper appreciation for life after my sexual assault. Over time, I learned to be proud of my colorful wings. I desperately wanted this same experience for others who found themselves thrust into the confusion of the chrysalis after sexual assault.

The ribbon-cutting ceremony at the Butterfly House remains one of the best days of my life. The sun was shining, and the air was light and crisp.

The executive director of the Florida Council Against Sexual Violence (FCASV), Jennifer Dritt, flew down from Tallahassee and spoke at the event. As a user of FCASV's website and services during my healing, I personally appreciated her kind words and assurances that the new RCC would have a significant impact on the healing and safety of those living in Palm Beach County.

All of the community partners who made the dream a reality were there as well, in addition to my family members, the media, and hospital staff. We gave several tours of the Butterfly House that morning to local television and newspapers so that they could get the word out to the general public about the amazing comprehensive services now available to victims of sexual assault.

Ever since that emotional opening day in December 2011, the Butterfly House has remained my most enduring project. In the beginning, Jamie and I stocked the center using the money that we personally set aside each year for charitable contributions. As word spread throughout the community about the Butterfly House, however, the number of rape survivors seen each year steadily increased. While the growth was a cause for great celebration, Jamie and I could no longer sustain the Butterfly House solely through our own personal contributions. The need had outgrown our capacity.

Instead, we set up a small nonprofit 501(c)(3) called the Not Just Me Foundation to help with purchasing clothes, toiletries, food, and other comfort care items for each survivor that came through the doors. I quickly became that annoying friend and neighbor who would ask people for ten- to fifteen-dollar contributions to clothe and feed a survivor in the community. I am still that person today, as every passing year has resulted in an increase in survivors seeking help.

It is important to note that while crime itself is not necessarily increasing in our area, awareness of the issue and the demand for comprehensive care are up. Prior to the opening of the Butterfly House, Palm Beach County provided services to about 250 survivors of sexual violence a year. Once we formed the SART, that number increased to over 700 survivors per year before COVID.

These numbers are empirical proof that the Butterfly House has made a substantial impact on the welfare of our county's citizens. Crime victims need, and want, a compassionate, coordinated response. I promised county administrators back on day one that, "if you build it, they will come." It wasn't a slogan—it was a responsibility. I'm glad the promise rang true, and our citizens are all better protected.

27

From Local to Global

FOR THE NEXT FEW years, as the Butterfly House caught on locally and the SAFER Act started to make an impact across the country, my attention turned to advancing statewide initiatives in Florida. I thought long and hard about who else might benefit from hearing a survivor's voice and prayed that God would continue to open doors for advocacy.

It became a mutually beneficial mission. I found great healing in connecting with the types of providers that aided in my recovery and, as a reflex, hoped to expand and improve services for others. I kept asking myself: *Who could I speak to next?*

The answer came quickly when I was contacted by a nursing coordinator at the previously mentioned FCASV. The state coalition had implemented a program to increase the number of forensic nurses or SANEs in Florida and asked if I would participate in the training. Of course, the answer was yes. I realized fast that if we wanted better outcomes for survivors, the first point of medical contact mattered just as much as policy. That realization made the invitation from FCASV feel less like an opportunity and more like a responsibility.

SANE nursing is something I feel very strongly about, and yet it is a field of care many people are largely unaware of. Before my rape, I had no idea that specialized sexual assault nurses even existed or were so vital to the overall physical and emotional health of a victim. Now, in hindsight, I know my personal interactions with a SANE set the tone for everything else that came after.

When creating the Butterfly House, I feel that hiring certified SANEs was the most important element we included. It was crucial to our mission that the medical professionals interfacing with our victims have specialized knowledge of the uniquely sensitive nature of sexual assault crimes and hopefully minimize the retraumatization of their patients.

Through the FCASV training, I was able to share with aspiring SANEs how crucial their job is and the positive influence they can have on an individual survivor's journey. Before too long, I found myself doing these trainings all over the state and speaking at national forensic nursing conferences about how we built a successful forensic exam center in Palm Beach County.

In addition to stressing the importance of compassionate medical care, I also talked with them about the critical role SANEs play in a survivor's fight for justice. A nurse's attention to detail in reports, their diligent collection of DNA evidence from the body, and expert testimony during trial are crucial when a sexual assault case finally sees the inside of a courtroom.

As much as compassionate medical care can stabilize a survivor physically and mentally, I knew it was only one part of the complex equation. Healing and justice also depend on how survivors are treated by law enforcement in the earliest moments after an assault. I started doing a similar kind of training for police departments.

Every year on the anniversary of my assault, especially in the early years, I sent emails to the detectives involved in my case to express my gratitude for the wonderful job they did sustaining me and helping me get justice. One year, the lead detective in my case sent an email back to me and asked if I had any interest in coming to speak to new road patrol officers at the Miami-Dade Police Department. Again, I jumped at the chance.

The police in Miami really seemed to appreciate hearing from a local survivor, and they gave me several additional opportunities to come back and talk again and again about the value of a trauma-informed approach. Eventually, I did similar training in West Palm Beach to remind local officers about the new Butterfly House protocols and why everyone benefits from victims being taken to a rape crisis center instead of the local hospital. I felt like I had found my calling and agreed to speak to any group that reached out, no matter where.

What began as informal conversations with local officers quietly gathered momentum. Before I fully understood what was happening, the work was no longer confined to Florida. I suddenly found myself giving presentations to all kinds of audiences about the "survivor experience."

In 2012, I was unexpectedly invited to present in Carbondale, Illinois, at a prosecutor-based training held by the Illinois Victim Assistants' Association. It was my first time taking the law enforcement/advocate piece of the story so far away from home. What was most incredible about the experience was that the synergy was so palpable. We were able to share new ways to solve common problems experienced by survivors and troubleshoot old ways of trying to get them more involved.

We set up friendships and informal alliances where help and support among agencies could be accessed easily across state lines with just a call or a text. That experience in Illinois marked a turning point for me. It confirmed that the survivor voice wasn't just welcome—it was absolutely needed far beyond the communities I knew and lived in.

The thrill of this cooperative experience made me want to set up more seminars for providers. Fortunately, word-of-mouth helped, and I started getting emails from agencies all over the US asking me to come and volunteer to tell my story. I started with State Attorney training in several judicial circuits across Florida, talking to a combined audience of officers and lawyers from the Florida Keys to the Panhandle.

By the time 2016 rolled around, I was getting calls for law enforcement and judicial training presentations from places like Las Vegas, Colorado Springs, Albuquerque, and Ontario, Canada. There was a willingness in communities to start using more trauma-informed techniques with survivors, as well as a growing acceptance by police departments that rapists could no longer be stereotyped during investigations.

As I spoke to more professionals across the country, one truth kept surfacing again and again: Our systems were failing not because of a lack of effort, but because of deeply ingrained assumptions about who commits rape—and where danger lives.

Part of the evil found in rape crimes is the ability of the perpetrator to metamorphose into whatever form they need to assume in order to become an invisible predator moving between worlds. Months of time in my investigation were lost chasing a supposed inner-city, ex-con, high school dropout, with a mom involved in prostitution and a nameless father. I don't know if the investigators would have ever thought to look for a local family man who grew up in an upper-middle-class neighborhood, attended an excellent high school, and was the son of a federal agent who professed Christian values and had close involvement with the church. It just seemed truly incongruous.

Society needed a better approach to identifying predators and anticipating where they were hunting. It was no longer just in the dark, in the shadows, in the middle of the night. It was in broad daylight, at churches and in preschool parking lots. These perpetrators were bold, empowered, and more depraved than ever. It strengthened my resolve that DNA was, and still is, the best way to identify and catch the worst offenders in society. Evil could no longer be stereotyped. Science had to step in.

28

The Call from the State Department

FROM 2014 TO 2016, I found myself thrust into another life-changing project that I never would have dreamed of. This one stemmed from my days advocating for the SAFER Act in Washington, DC. Just as I do now, I ended my presentations on Capitol Hill during that time by offering to personally meet with anyone who has ideas or concerns about how we as a nation can help survivors of rape and eradicate sexual violence in communities.

Someone in the audience during my testimony remembered this and actually gave me a call. They said they were reaching out on behalf of the State Department. Immediately after our hellos, I started pinching myself while mentally preparing for any mission they wanted to send my way.

In hindsight, the call made sense. The same survivor-centered approach I had been speaking about across the United States was now being sought on a much larger stage. During that initial conversation with the woman on the phone, I learned that she was calling me from the International Association of the Chiefs of Police (IACP), the world's largest and most influential professional association for law enforcement officials around the globe.

Headquartered just outside of Washington, DC, the IACP is a nonprofit organization known for its commitment to working with various international agencies to enhance community safety and address the most pressing threats to security around the world. In the United States, the IACP often partners with the Department of Justice and the US State Department, offering law enforcement training to agencies that may be in need.

This time, the IACP reached out for help in cooperation with the State Department, hoping to put a comprehensive program in place to combat sexual and gender-based violence (SGBV) in Egypt. To understand why Egypt became the focus of this effort, it helps to look at what that country was facing at the time.

Beginning as early as 2007, the United States Bureau of International Narcotics and Law Enforcement Affairs (INL) within the State Department began working more closely with leaders in Cairo to calm the political instability in the nation, which had long been characterized by single-party authoritarian rule. After the first democratic election in 2011 and until the 2013 military coup, the partnership was able to lower the rate of general crime in the region.

Unfortunately, SGBV in particular was rising during this period, and there were no significant plans in place to effectively ease the suffering of women and girls in Egypt. This did not go unnoticed by agencies such as the United Nations Office on Drugs and Crime (UNDOC). In 2013, the issue of preventing SGBV started gaining more traction inside certain agencies in Egypt.

The expressed goal of the State Department's branch of the INL is to provide improvements in the rule of law and protections for human rights through criminal justice sector development. INL programs build capacity to conduct effective criminal investigations, including independently analyzing physical evidence and respecting the rights of victims. This mission, in conjunction with the increasing

SGBV in Egypt, made for a suitable match. The collaborative project took root quickly.

In 2014, several members of the Egyptian Judicial Authority and the IACP arranged the first study tour for Egyptian officials to come to the United States and learn how sexual crimes can be investigated and prosecuted in order to collectively protect community safety and secure justice for victims. Much to my delight, the trip would be run through a partnership with the Miami-Dade Police Department.

The ten Egyptian officials from Cairo selected for the program visited the member agencies of the Miami-Dade County SART, including the RCC, police headquarters, DNA lab, as well as advocacy and justice centers. While the study tours were designed to share investigative and medical best practices, the organizers believed that hearing directly from a survivor would humanize the training in a way policy alone could not—an insight that would soon place me at the center of the project.

I became directly involved in the project during the second study tour in late 2014, when another small group of officials from Cairo came to Miami for training. After doing a little independent research about why sexual assault is so severely underreported in Egypt, I grew quite nervous about getting up and telling my story to the all-male audience.

In Egypt, speaking about sexuality and personal health issues in a mixed-gender environment is discouraged. The culture, deeply rooted in conservative and traditional norms, makes any discourse about the harsh realities of rape and its aftermath difficult to discuss openly. This silence is not accidental—it is systemic, and is a huge factor in why change regarding SGBV is so tough to accomplish.

As expected, it was extremely uncomfortable for me to open up to the group about what I had experienced during my assaults—especially without using the anatomically correct words for body parts and fluids. Instead of skirting around the ugliness of the crimes, however, I decided to be very candid about what happened to me. I chose honesty over comfort.

I could feel the room cringe repeatedly as I described the rapes and how my perpetrator attempted to evade detection. About halfway through, I became concerned that the participants might stop listening to me or condemn me for being vulgar. The familiar fear crept in—that telling the truth might cost me credibility instead of boosting it. I felt vulnerable and naked all over again.

After my presentation finished, however, the response I received was very different from the one I had braced myself for. They did not sit quietly. No one reprimanded me for my frank language. Rather, the attendees stood and applauded, asking many questions about my healing. They were curious about where I found the courage to stand and speak out in the wake of such an attack.

I told them the truth. My strength came from my God, my family, and the team of professionals in Miami that supported me and fought for me from that first 9-1-1 call all the way through to the sentencing. I was still standing because they refused to let me stand and suffer alone.

As the conversations deepened, cultural differences around justice and accountability began to surface in unexpected ways. Punitive concepts that felt absolute to me, I learned, were not universally agreed upon.

One of the conversations that shocked me the most had to do with my perpetrator's sentencing; instead of being impressed, as I have always been, by the seven life sentences my rapist was given by the state of Florida, several participants questioned if I would feel more satisfied if he had been executed. In Egypt, that would have been his sentence. I was honest with them and said that I had never thought about the death penalty being a punishment for rape.

In the US, we are taught that the death penalty is more of an "eye for an eye" situation. When you take a life, the state is sometimes justified in taking your life as punishment in return. Not all murders qualify for capital punishment, however. It is reserved for only the most heinous killings. In America, incarceration is the most acceptable form of retribution.

I explained that I had closure with the seven life sentences, and that closure is what helped me heal. The closure came from a combination of being believed by law enforcement, consistently supported by advocacy networks, and by the judicial system holding him accountable for what he had done.

Saying that out loud helped me reaffirm for myself something deeply personal: Even if the death of my rapist was an option for justice, it would not be enough to erase all of the pain and anguish my family endured. The trauma of rape deeply affects both the body and the mind. And while the wounds of the flesh eventually heal, I am forced to live every day with the psychological impacts of his crimes. His death will never alleviate the pain of some of those wounds.

I said confidently that the kind of closure I received through his trial and sentencing, however, gave me the ability to function and move forward. That is what I want for all victims of violence: the opportunity to be heard, believed, and for the severity of the crime to be fully acknowledged.

I found an increased sense of security in his conviction and punishment, but I know now that my path to freedom began earlier than the final verdict. It started when my community gave me the opportunity to heal out loud and did not minimize my pain.

After that second contingent of Egyptians left, many reached out and thanked me for my bravery and honesty. I went on to deliver that presentation to all of the remaining groups that traveled from Egypt to the United States, both down in Miami-Dade County and then later in cooperation with the Colorado Springs Police Department.

In total, more than 50 law enforcement, medical, and judicial officials traveled from Egypt to the United States on those study tours to learn about the importance of victim-centered care. I was proud to be able to accompany them in person to some of the local agencies that had been crucial to my survival. Every group responded to the story of the crimes against me in a similar fashion and asked many of the same questions about the investigation and healing process.

Along the way, I made friends with dozens of the participants, exchanging promises to stay in touch. At the time, I didn't yet realize that these study tours were only the beginning—or that I would soon be asked to take this work halfway around the world.

29

Survivor-Led Reform

IN OCTOBER 2016, A few days before the anniversary of my family's abduction, I received an invitation to travel with the IACP team to Cairo for the opening of the country's first SGBV forensic exam center in November. I was speechless. I could not believe they wanted me to fly to the other side of the world and talk about what happened to me before even larger groups of people. This meant that the message about support, forensics, and justice was being heard and that real change was happening.

My soul delighted in the fact that I was asked to present my story alongside a skilled forensic nurse, a prosecutor, an advocate, and two law enforcement officers who had been working on the collaborative project from the start. In an unexpected way, it made me feel like a legitimate professional voice in the room and not just a volunteer with a tragic story.

The invitation confirmed that my lived experiences with violence had tangible value. It provided a sense of validation that I possess a specific kind of knowledge that can be helpful for others around the world. It's not the kind of knowledge or insight that can be taught theoretically out of a textbook, but rather the kind of knowledge acquired through personally confronting real-world challenges and inspiring others to rethink their own systems and evolve. I wasn't simply a crime victim; I was a survivor with a blueprint for change.

The invitation to Cairo felt like a natural continuation of everything that had come before—local reform, national legislation, and international study tours now converging into a single moment. After a couple of days of protocol training in late October 2016, our group departed Washington, DC, for Cairo.

We were swept up into a whirlwind of activity as soon as we touched down on Egyptian soil. We were only going to be there for five days and had so much to accomplish. The energy in the city was electrifying. The sights, sounds, and smells dwarfed anything I had experienced in America. It felt like New York City on steroids.

Our first day was the only time during the trip that we had for sightseeing and acclimating, so we hit all of the highlights at warp speed. Our group visited ancient mosques, rode camels, and ate traditional Egyptian food like koshary. We saw the Sphinx and marvelled at the pyramids. I even overcame my intense claustrophobia and journeyed deep inside the tiny passageways of the Great Pyramid into the upper room.

We went to the famed open-air markets and haggled with locals selling spices, lamps, and papyrus. It was a true adventure that exceeded my expectations. As extraordinary as those moments were, however, we were acutely aware that we were not there as tourists. The heart of the trip lay in the work we had come to do.

Our days in Cairo were dedicated to making presentations about the importance of each member of a SART and how coordination between agencies, from start to finish, can produce stronger survivors and safer communities. All of the meetings were held at the hotel to minimize our travel around the city. When we did travel, it was with members of the American Embassy staff in armored vehicles. Although I was aware of the crime statistics and the political unrest, I felt safe while I was in the country and appreciated the Egyptians' generosity and hospitality.

The best part of the project was seeing how the study tours in the US, combined with the continued contact between individuals in both countries, led to a deeper and more authentic understanding of the complexities of sexual violence—and the shared responsibility to address it. In the years we spent working together, it never felt to me like one government telling another government what to do. Rather, it felt like groups of humans sharing experiences and learning together about how to handle the universal evil known as rape. It renewed my hope in humanity.

We were joined daily by the head of the Egyptian Forensic Medicine Authority (FMA), Dr. Hishram Abdul Hamid. His ongoing commitment to the project was truly beautiful, and I personally felt a great amount of support from him. One morning in Cairo, he gifted each of us with an engraved gold shield from the government and said kind words about what we each brought to the success of the project. I will hold his words in my heart, always.

Despite the warmth I found in all of my interactions with my new Egyptian friends, the day of my presentation still filled me with dread. I was anxious about everything. I hoped that I was dressed appropriately (a pantsuit with a turtleneck) and prayed that the audience of close to 200 professionals from Egypt's medical, judicial, and women's advocacy sectors would hear what I was saying and be moved to action.

I had been warned early on in the trip that, due to the frank subject matter and the presence of both men and women in the audience, some people might walk out when I started speaking, and others might even spit on me while I was talking. As soon as I loaded up my presentation and my children's innocent faces appeared on the screen, however, I became more resolute than ever before to speak the grisly truth about sexual violence.

I am delighted to say that no one left the room while I spoke, and nobody spat on me as they exited. Instead, about 98 percent of the audience stood and clapped.

In the end, I was proud that I had faced my fears and spoken about the ugliness of rape and the long, very personal road to healing.

After I concluded my talk, a few professional women approached me in private and via email to disclose their own stories of sexual violence and the intense pain they have carried with them over the years. I was stunned by how open they were with me.

The audience was grateful for our entire US team and the work everyone did to change minds, hearts, and protocols in Egypt. By the conclusion of the two-year IACP project, those shifts were no longer theoretical—they were measurable.

Some of the changes that emerged included:

- Buy-in from key stakeholders, including representatives from the National Council for Women, the Ministry of Health, the Ministry of Interior, and the Ministry of Justice.
- Modified forensic evidentiary protocols to minimize contamination during the collection process.
- Twenty-four-hour hotline services—advertised on public posters, with Facebook and YouTube links.
- A modern forensic exam clinic in Cairo, equipped with a colposcope and a private waiting room.
- Plans for new forensic exam clinics to open in Alexandria and other cities, including expansion into rural areas.

- An increased acceptance that sexual assault may be a legal finding, without evidence of trauma or need for virginity testing (a significant philosophical shift).
- The classification of female genital mutilation as a felony rather than a misdemeanor.
- Increased discussion between the forensics team and prosecutors to ensure that formal requests for evidence collection are broad enough to include a thorough exam and that exams are done expeditiously and respectfully.
- Discussion of designating female officers in each police district to serve as an initial point of advocacy in SGBV cases.
- Discussion of short-term and long-term goals that address the implementation of memoranda of understanding (MOUs) and legislative amendments to recognize and establish formal SART, including multijurisdictional collaboration between agencies.
- Implementation of educational programs geared toward young adults, spotlighting awareness of SGBV and promoting women's independence and strength.

I am happy to say that the momentum from the project is still alive today, and I have had the wonderful opportunity to meet up with my Egyptian friends at international conferences over the years. While challenges certainly persist, the seeds of change were planted during the project.

Recent international publications report that medical professionals have since received specialized training on forensic exams through the UNODC, clinics have spread to cities outside of Cairo and into some rural areas, and the issues of SGBV prevention and follow-up care for victims remain active topics of conversation.

Not long after this chapter closed in Egypt, another opportunity for international advocacy became available. This time, the work would be a little closer to home in the state of Jalisco, Mexico. In mid-2017, the IACP called and asked if I would like to be part of an SBGV project in Guadalajara, Mexico, that was similar to the one we had done in Egypt. This project would be a collaboration between the US State Department, the Attorney General's Office of the State of Jalisco, and The Center for Women's Justice located in Guadalajara. As I am sure they expected, I immediately confirmed my participation.

I was thrilled to reunite with several of my closest friends from the Egypt trip and excited to meet a few new ones who were already leading the fight against SGBV in both the US and Mexico. For this project, I would be part of the US team presenting workshops to law enforcement officers, rape and domestic violence crisis centers, and advocacy programs throughout the state. The project would culminate in a final symposium held in December 2017.

The project in Mexico was extremely compelling because it incorporated programming about the distinct and often overlooked connection between domestic violence and sexual violence. My lived experience and advocacy over the years have proven to me that the two are inextricably linked.

A sexual predator is the same beast, whether they assault individuals they know and purport to love or attack complete strangers on the street. Ignoring the scourge of sexual violence that is present in interpersonal relationships and treating it as a "lesser crime" than when it happens to a stranger is blatantly unjust and dangerous for society.

I loved the enthusiasm in Guadalajara and their commitment to provide better training and resources on both types of violence. Being able to tour the centers and witness individuals and families receiving care is something I will remember forever.

Once again, similar to the project in Egypt, the process of sharing stories and making human connections in safe spaces was what moved the needle of change for everyone. Across borders, languages, and legal systems, one truth remained constant: Survivor-led reform works when people are willing to listen—and when systems are brave enough to change.

30

Florida Counts the Kits

BIG LEGISLATIVE CHANGES WERE happening in the US during these years as well. While my advocacy had expanded internationally, the ripple effects of the SAFER Act were quietly reshaping justice efforts back home. After the SAFER Act passed and became part of the 2013 reauthorization of the Violence Against Women Act (VAWA), states became eligible to apply for new federal grants to conduct audits designed to identify and count the number of untested sexual assault kits in their jurisdiction.

In late 2013, Rebecca O'Connor, the Vice President of Public Policy for RAINN, invited me to join a small group of survivor-advocates, and together we formed the Rape Kit Action Project (RKAP). There were about a dozen of us, each selected from the various national sexual assault advocacy groups we were affiliated with. I vividly remember our first meeting in Washington, DC, that fall. We all came from different states and had distinctly different experiences with our own rape kit testing and pursuit of justice.

What became clear very quickly was that this was no longer about individual stories—it was about a systemic failure we were uniquely positioned to confront together. For days, as we listened and shared, a fire began to burn among us, and we realized that together we had the potential to drive meaningful change— to start changing DNA testing laws in every state across the country.

As part of our meeting in Washington, DC, we were given a guided tour of a company called Bode Technology (Bode), headquartered in nearby Lorton, Virginia, which had lent its support to the RKAP. Over its 30-year history, Bode has become the largest private forensic DNA analysis laboratory in America, providing state-of-the-art DNA analysis services to law enforcement, crime labs, attorneys, and government agencies worldwide. It is interesting to note that the company was one of the primary national laboratories tasked with testing and identifying severely damaged human remains from the 9/11 attacks.

We went to Bode that fall day in 2013 ostensibly to learn about the company but, more importantly, to see how they were working to reduce the nation's backlog of unprocessed rape kits. When we got there, our tour guides thanked us all in advance for our public advocacy regarding the backlog.

At that time, the American public was still largely unaware of this escalating crisis in the criminal justice system. Our RKAP group listened to presentations and took an extensive tour of the facilities. We saw large scientific labs where analysts, dressed in full protective gear, were processing rape kits using cutting-edge technologies.

What still haunts me the most from that tour was what happened next, in the moments when the guides allowed us to see the interior of one of Bode's giant storage facilities. Inside that space were large boxes filled with rape kits, each numbered and in an individual envelope. The boxes were completely full and sat on huge industrial shelving units, organized in rows that reached from floor to ceiling.

Thousands and thousands of rape kits were just sitting there in silence. It felt like I was in a horrifying maze of suspended justice.

Reading about the backlog was heartbreaking, but witnessing a slice of it in person was almost soul-crushing.

I could not believe that each of the rape kits awaiting testing was obtained from a sexual assault victim just like me. Every kit held biological evidence from their bodies, evidence crucial to justice and healing. Swabs from their terror sat there in stacks, one on top of another.

As I began to tear up over what I was witnessing, I reminded myself that the fact that they were even at a testing facility at all was a positive sign. At least now, the rape kits were in line waiting for their turn to be seen and no longer hidden away in a drawer or brushed aside—much like many of the victims they represented. I framed the photo I took that day of the endless rows of untested evidence. They say that a "picture is worth a thousand words"—or in this case, the identities of thousands of perpetrators.

The memories I have of that day at Bode are imprinted in my mind forever. I still hold on to them tightly and use them as a primary source of inspiration for all the work I have done, and continue to do, on forensic DNA identification in America and around the world.

I think taking all of us to the lab was a brilliant motivator, galvanizing the RKAP women to return to our home states and advocate for change. At the meeting in Washington, DC, we were privileged to meet with Ilse Knecht from the National Center for Victims of Crime and Lisa Hurst from an established Washington, DC-based policy agency. Both women are treasure troves of information on how to get the attention of state lawmakers and effectively educate them on the crucial importance of rape kit reform.

Their passion was contagious, and I immediately put them both on my speed dial. After all, as soon as I returned to Florida, there was going to be work to do to get my home state up and running with an audit to count the true number of Florida's backlogged rape kits. It was finally time to use the SAFER Act grants that I helped fight for.

Ilse, now at the Joyful Heart Foundation, helped guide me to the appropriate state leaders who would be willing to listen to the idea of putting measures in place to get the count started in Florida. She shared talking points and provided government offices with links to excellent resources from other states that had also conducted audits.

Asking any state to complete this kind of meticulous task, one that requires buy-in from law enforcement and other major stakeholders, is not an easy job at all. No agency wants to scour their office looking for unprocessed forensic kits and have to publicly claim accountability for adding to the backlog. However, through grit, education, and relentless letter writing and meetings, Florida got the job done.

The audit passed as state law SB2500. I was a bit stunned when the results of the audit revealed a much higher number of sexual assault kits than I had suspected, especially as a survivor whose kit was processed at a lab in Miami with no sizable backlog at the time of my crime. Things had changed significantly in the state since 2002. In the years since my assault, the system had quietly slipped into crisis.

When the official audit numbers were publicly announced in late 2015, the Florida Department of Law Enforcement (FDLE) reported that they were in possession of 13,435 untested rape kits across the state's 279 participating agencies. Once case reviews were finished, it was determined that while a smaller percentage of kits fell under allowable exceptions for non-testing, 9,484 of the kits were actually required to be sent out for lab analysis under agency guidelines.

After the media began to expose the issue, people across Florida became outraged. How could the state hold back justice for so many of its citizens over the years? It looked like neglect, plain and simple. And, the human cost of that neglect was devastating.

Many people I connected with after the audit tearfully spoke of years, and sometimes decades, wasted living in fear as they waited for their perpetrator to be identified. Most assumed that the reason they never heard back from the police was that their kit was tested, but had simply not produced a DNA match in the system

Survivors were deeply frustrated to learn that while they personally struggled for years with crippling anxiety and a lack of closure, the agencies they relied on for justice had not even submitted their kits for testing. Instead, the evidence taken from their bodies had been cast aside, left to collect dust on shelves.

Calling the backlog a tragedy feels inadequate. It was a prolonged failure that compounded trauma and silently denied thousands of survivors the dignity of their rapes being taken seriously.

31

Test All Kits

ALMOST IMMEDIATELY AFTER THE shocking audit report was released, the momentum in advocacy shifted toward writing adequate legislation to prevent the problem from happening again. Exposure had done its work; now accountability demanded action.

The momentum was there for change, and now, when I spoke to government officials and community leaders about drafting new laws, it felt noticeably easier. The backlog was no longer an abstract concept that I was touting. I had seen it up close and was armed with the numbers to empirically prove its existence.

I also had documented data and information from state law enforcement agencies and labs explaining why it happened in the first place. For the first time, the conversation was no longer about whether reform was necessary; it was about how quickly it could be achieved.

I am happy to say that before too long, a workable legislative plan was proposed. Senator Lizbeth Benacquisto, who had been our legislative warrior pushing for the creation of the Butterfly House in Palm Beach County five years earlier, sponsored the mandatory testing bill in the Senate alongside Representative Janet Adkins in the House of Representatives. In February 2016, the bill, simply known as SB 636, passed unanimously in both chambers.

According to the new bill, the decision to test rape kits would no longer be left up to the discretion of local agencies. Law enforcement would now be required to submit all rape kits collected from victims in their jurisdiction to the crime lab within thirty days of acquiring them. Rape kits could no longer be set aside or delayed for subjective reasons once they entered into custody. Once submitted to the lab, all kits must be handled in an expedient manner, and a report must be generated within 120 days.

This shift marked a fundamental change in how Florida viewed sexual assault evidence, moving away from treating it as optional, inconvenient, or conditional, and recognizing it as essential. Because of SB636, survivors in Florida would no longer find themselves waiting years for results or wondering if their evidence had made it to the lab in the first place. At the heart of the law was a distinct message: *Every kit matters. Timely identification matters. All survivors count.*

The legislation also shifted the system's focus towards a more victim-centered approach, as individuals would now be informed of their rights regarding rape kit testing during their exam. This requirement promoted greater accountability and transparency within Florida's justice system by establishing clear expectations for the handling of future sexual assault evidence.

Still, one critical question remained unanswered: What would be done about all of the untested kits discovered through the audit? Thousands of victims in the state were still waiting for their opportunity for closure. Fortunately, written directly into the new law was a deadline for law enforcement to submit a plan to the governor's office to eradicate the existing backlog. Reform would not be theoretical. It would be measured, enforced, and completed.

On March 24, 2016, I proudly stood next to Florida Governor Rick Scott and alongside Florida Attorney General Pam Bondi as he signed SB636 into state law. It was one of the most memorable moments of my "new" life. Yet the true impact of the law would not be felt on the day it was signed; it would be revealed in the years that followed.

Within three years of passing the bill, Florida officially announced that it had completely cleared the backlog of rape kits uncovered during the 2015 audit. Out of the 13,435 previously unprocessed kits identified statewide, 8,023 kits contained usable DNA profiles eligible for upload into the Combined DNA Index System (CODIS) maintained by the Federal Bureau of Investigation (FBI). When the upload was complete, an astounding 1,814 matches were identified in the database. The results were extraordinary.

Those numbers were not just statistics; they represented answers long denied. With close to 2,000 criminal profiles positively identified, Florida became a measurably safer place. More importantly, thousands of survivors were finally given what had been withheld for years: the possibility of truth, accountability, and closure.

My involvement with the bill was surprisingly cathartic, another reminder for me that God had been present in every step in my journey, even when I could not see it at the time. In hindsight, the whole experience seemed to be a beautiful example of the powerful words found in Genesis 50:20, "You intended to harm me, but God intended it for good to accomplish what is now being done, the saving of many lives" (NIV). There is a higher purpose in the pain my family endured. That truth does not erase what was lost, but it redeems it. That stirs hope in my heart and fuels my soul. It gives meaning to the suffering and provides the strength to continue the work.

32

Gail's Law

FAST FORWARD TO MAY 14, 2021, and I find myself standing outside of the Victim's Services office in West Palm Beach, with the media, state legislative representatives, and a brave woman named Gail Gardner. We were all there celebrating the passage of another pillar of rape kit reform in Florida. More specifically, the state's decision to implement a rape kit tracking system.

My own passion for tracking systems began a decade earlier, when I became involved with the SAFER Act in Congress in 2011. I advocated for tracking for months on Capitol Hill before the federal bill was pared down to include just rape kit testing timelines and processes to clear the existing backlog.

Long before tracking pizza orders or Amazon packages became standard, the concept of tracking rape kits felt obvious to me. Why shouldn't states be required to place a barcode on this crucial evidence to increase transparency in the process and restore a measure of control to survivors after such an invasive forensic examination? It's their body, their biological evidence, their story.

Despite its simplicity, the idea of rape kit tracking stalled for years. I started talking about the idea of tracking rape kits again while I worked on audit and testing legislation in Florida. I knew that despite my best rhetoric, logic alone was not going to be enough to resurrect the concept. Progress would require a significant human catalyst: a face, a name, and a story powerful enough to cut through institutional inertia.

The idea of tracking rape kits would not take on significant momentum until Gail's incredible story hit the news several years later. Her story became the human proof of what happens when evidence disappears inside a system with no accountability, and what becomes possible when that system is finally forced to respond.

In 2019, when the rape kit backlog had finally been cleared due to the "Test All Kits" law I helped pass in 2016, the state started to uncover stories of sexual assault survivors who had been denied timely justice. Gail was one of the many survivors who had been left behind.

In 1988, as a single mother of two children in Central Florida, she became the victim of a home invasion and brutal rape at the hands of a stranger. Gail reported the rape to the police and had a forensic exam done at a hospital. Afterward, she waited every day for answers, living in constant fear and assuming that her attacker had simply never been identified due to a lack of evidence. What Gail did not know, and had no way of knowing, was that the system she trusted had failed her almost immediately.

All this time, however, her rape kit sat on a shelf collecting dust in police storage. Early on in the investigation, it was cast aside. At the time of her assault, no one deemed her kit worthy enough to send for testing. For more than three decades, justice was not merely delayed for Gail. It was denied.

The 2016 legislation, coupled with advances in DNA technology, thankfully breathed new life into Gail's case, and her assailant was finally identified. After waiting more than 30 years to learn his name, a match in CODIS positively linked the DNA from her rape to a man named George Girtman. Also known as the "Malibu Rapist," Girtman was a serial offender already serving two life sentences in Florida for multiple sexual assaults. The truth that emerged was devastating, yet deeply illuminating.

The DNA identification made through the eventual testing of Gail's kit connected him to dozens of other sexual crimes, some of which involved victims who had died without ever knowing who their attacker was.

In 2021, Girtman was rearrested for Gail's rape and the assaults of six additional women in the 1980s and 1990s. What had once been dismissed as a single, unsolvable crime was revealed to be part of a much larger pattern, one that the system had failed to interrupt.

It was a triumphant moment in July 2024 when Gail and several other survivors summoned all of their strength and gave their victim impact statements at his trial. For many, it marked the first time their voices were formally acknowledged by the justice system. But Gail's courage did not stop at the courtroom.

Having lived for more than three decades knowing her rape kit had been pushed aside and forgotten, Gail was determined to make sure no survivor would ever endure the same silence. That resolve led her to fight hard for the creation of Gail's Law, the Florida legislation that mandates a statewide system for tracking rape kits and ensures survivors receive timely status updates about their cases.

Gail's case became a quintessential example for lawmakers, finally allowing them to see what advocates like me have known for a long time: Rapists are often serial offenders and rarely strike just once. It also powerfully affirmed the need for the 2016 "Test All Kits" legislation, which eliminated selective bias from the process.

For decades, rapists exploited the flaws in the system that created the backlog in the first place. While remaining free in their communities, they continued to victimize countless innocent people and operate with little fear of getting caught. Florida, along with dozens of other states, is safer today because of survivor-inspired laws.

33

What Now?

HOLDING FAST TO THE promise I made to God on the floor of my minivan in October 2002, I have continued to walk through every door that He has opened for me. Regardless of whether that door is to a coffee shop where a survivor, nurse, or advocate wants to share their personal struggles, or the door opens to a convention center packed with government officials or DNA analysts, I go. I trust that God will place me wherever I am needed and will calm my fears.

While it is often physically and mentally draining to retell the story of the crime and its aftermath, in the last few years, I have only intensified my pace. I return emails every week to professionals in a variety of different fields nationwide who reach out with questions or invitations for me to help them improve the survivor experience. What began as survival eventually became stewardship.

Since the beginning of my advocacy more than fifteen years ago, I have volunteered to speak to groups of individuals involved in every stage of a survivor's SART journey. This work first began with law enforcement officers in South Florida, encouraging them to adopt a more victim-centered response to sex crimes. Over the years, that reach has steadily expanded to include police departments in other states.

For example, every six months for the last five years, I have travelled to Albuquerque, New Mexico, to help with their detective academies. I always look forward to participating in their training program, and after all of this time, the people who are in charge of it are now like family to me. I feel like we are all equally invested in the mission to make New Mexico a safer place.

Not every state has the same laws or resources for survivors, and many departments are eager to improve on that. I relish the opportunity to encourage law enforcement in their jobs and help push for change. But law enforcement reform is only one piece of the complex puzzle of criminal justice.

I also have a strong desire to promote advances in DNA technology and share with lab analysts how important their work is in a survivor's healing. Because the people who work in the field of DNA rarely have direct contact with victims, I enjoy meeting with them and thanking them for everything they do to help individuals get justice for these intimate crimes. Their scientific role in processing and interpreting the forensic evidence is a fundamental building block in criminal cases.

Work at the labs is very tedious, so it is extremely important to me that the scientists know how much value they bring to the process. Every sample they analyze is critical in either identifying or exonerating someone connected to a life-altering crime. I feel like my DNA analyst quite literally saved my life. I tell them at the end of every presentation that if they are ever tempted to quit because they don't see the difference they are making in the world, they should call me, and I will convince them to keep going.

Over time, my advocacy has expanded beyond professionals already in the field to those still preparing to enter it. What began as gratitude turned into mentorship and, eventually, into education. For almost a decade now, I have made presentations to future analysts at universities across the United States.

After I spoke at the International Symposium for Human Identification (ISHI) in Minneapolis in 2016, Dr. Daniele Podini from George Washington University's Graduate School of Forensic Science approached me about a collaboration. Dr. Podini wanted his students to know the real-world impact of their future profession and thought my story would be a good inspiration.

The plan he proposed was for his students to work on a fictitious case all semester and orally present their forensic findings to an audience as their final exam in May. The audience was supposed to simulate a lay jury, and the exercise was intended to be good practice for when they might be called as a witness in a future trial.

Of course, I immediately agreed to his proposal, and have flown to Washington, DC, for the last nine years to listen to the students' final projects. At the conclusion of each session, I reveal my identity as the real-life victim behind the case and explain just how critical an analyst's expert testimony can be in determining a verdict.

Some of my favorite blessings are the relationships I have kept with many of the former students, who continue to reach out and share updates about their careers, families, and lives beyond the lab.

I am passionate that research and funding for advances in DNA and other forensic technology should be a priority for everyone concerned about public safety and security in this country. Identifying perpetrators quickly and accurately is at the heart of the justice system. I know firsthand that no survivor wants to spend an extra minute of their life worrying about being revictimized or about the possibility of an innocent person being wrongfully incarcerated.

There is safety in science. True justice demands compassion, informed investigations, and, when available, objective scientific proof. I was lucky that in 2002, the Miami-Dade lab invested in the most cutting-edge technologies of the time. Being raped somewhere else in the country might not have produced the same verdict in the trial.

I delight in knowing that in the years since my family's abduction, innovations like rapid DNA technology at police stations and the analysis of transfer DNA from surfaces have led to an increase in the number of profiles being uploaded into CODIS. The rise of forensic investigative genetic genealogy (FIGG) is another remarkable tool that generates investigative leads and helps catch dangerous predators who often hide in plain sight.

Technological advances in cybercrime analysis and digital forensics are becoming more important than ever in solving individual cases and protecting future victims. My voice will always be available to support organizations committed to this type of scientific development.

I will also never stop fighting for increased medical and support resources for survivors. Every person on this planet deserves the right to heal from sexual violence. RCCs and SANEs should be accessible to everyone. The luck of geography should not determine who gets dignified medical care and the opportunity for justice. That is true both in the United States and around the globe.

The rate of sexual assault is simply too high for communities to ignore. I want to be a part of the network of survivors and advocates educating society about the invisible scars of violence. They can last a lifetime and be quite disabling for people trying to move past what happened to them.

Individuals who have been through sexual assault should feel confident that their community stands with them and is committed to making sure professional resources are available to help with complex psychological concerns, such as post-traumatic stress disorder, after their experience. No one should feel alone at any point in their healing journey. Isolation is the enemy of healing.

34

Reframing the Loss and Counting the Blessings

THERE'S NO WAY TO sugarcoat what happens to a person in the wake of sexual violence. The damage that sexual assault does to a person is inherently ugly and unfair. The reality of what life is like after rape is complex and, unfortunately, not something that goes away just because enough time has passed or your perpetrator is locked up.

Survivors of rape, whether the assault is reported or unreported, are essentially burdened with a life sentence of their own. They experience a future they did not ask for and pain no one deserves. No earthly form of justice can permanently take away that hurt or fade the scars.

In examining my own journey from survivor to advocate, I can clearly see now that some of the losses I experienced in my life after my rapes ended up being more painful than the violent act itself. Acknowledging those losses, grieving them, and rebuilding a new, more authentic normal is what has saved my sanity and allowed me to find joy again. It is another blessing born from my trauma.

Before my healing could begin, I had to name what had been taken from me. The first loss a sexual assault victim naturally experiences is the fundamental betrayal of trust by a fellow human being. It isn't an ordinary betrayal that comes from simple lies or deception.

Rather, it is one that originates in a perverse way, weaponizing human connection and destroying the autonomy of the soul. The psychological damage and physical pain of rape occur concurrently.

Rape takes the deepest act of personal connection two souls can experience and turns it into an act that dehumanizes one person and fills their body and mind with feelings of intense fear. The love and respect inherent in the concept of consent are replaced by hate and domination. It is natural to feel like you have been damaged down to your core and to believe you can never fully trust anyone again.

It's not your bike or wallet that was stolen during the crime. It was a part of your spirit that was taken, and there is no tangible way to replace that. For me, the only way to fill the void was to lean into God's promises and let my faith fill in the holes. Safety, once lost, must be relearned slowly and intentionally.

In the aftermath of violence, survivors may also experience a profound loss of personal safety and security. They may mourn the fact that while everything in their physical environment may be exactly the same, it will feel forever different. For me, this happened almost immediately.

As soon as I finished my rape exam and subsequent law enforcement interviews, the police dropped me back off at my childhood home. Just days prior, I had visited my parents there, and it felt secure and comfortable. My soul felt at peace inside the walls of the house. However, as soon as I walked through the front doors in the early morning hours of October 17, 2002, I suddenly felt like I didn't belong there. Everything about me felt off. It was as if I was viewing my presence there through a black and white carnival mirror.

I will never be able to feel the same way as I did when I visited the home before the rape, and I have grieved that. The same sense of displacement extended beyond the house and into the community itself. I learned, though, that I can truly love the space again.

This happened when I started experiencing new joys with my family there and reframed the location as the spot where my healing journey began. I replaced the pain with unbruised memories and a sense of gratitude. My old neighborhood supported me during my crisis and provided me with what I needed to move forward. Reminding myself of that makes me love Miami even more.

I experienced the same thing when I finally moved back into the home I shared with Jamie and the kids. My happy yellow house now seemed unsafe, and I saw shadows of my rapist around every corner and outside the windows. The innocence of childhood and the bliss of motherhood felt incongruous with the fear that followed me from room to room. Everything seemed strangely one-dimensional. I had tremendous trouble sleeping, and anxiety replaced the joy I once felt imagining our family's future there.

The day we decided to move, I felt like I lost another piece of my identity. Deep down, I think my mind finally surrendered to the fact that saying goodbye to our home was simply the price we were going to have to pay to give our kids a more carefree childhood. Heartbroken doesn't even begin to describe how I felt when we closed the front door for the last time and left Miami behind.

This was not the life we planned for. It was not what any of us would have chosen. At the time, it felt like revictimization. But I have come to love the town we landed in, and I know that choosing to start over allowed a great deal of healing to take place.

Other significant losses happened too, and, over time, they gave us a clearer perspective on life. Some of our core relationships with friends changed, and a few even ended. Over time, we learned that not everyone who was there for us at the beginning of the story would stick around until the end. It was an excruciatingly painful lesson.

I eventually stopped beating myself up over my feelings of abandonment and began to recognize that people fading away can just be part of human nature. Talking about violence is uncomfortable for most individuals. It isn't pleasant and requires people to acknowledge their own vulnerability. Individuals can love you and support you when your wounds are fresh, but may grow tired when they realize healing is an endurance run and not a sprint.

They may have loved the "old" you that was funny and carefree, the version of you that wasn't so messy and complicated. People often leave when their timeline says you should be "over it," even though, in theory, they know this is not the definition of unconditional love. This erosion of connection taught me something essential: How others respond to trauma can either compound the wound or become part of the healing.

Awkwardness starts to fill in the spaces where patience used to be. Trust me, no one is more aware of this than a survivor who realizes that sharing the struggles in their heart could mean abandonment by someone in their support system.

The bonds of friendship, or even family, can grow increasingly superficial for survivors. That is the point when many turn inward and begin detaching from their emotions. Self-isolation starts to happen even though the soul craves connection and trust. The world doesn't always consider that the survivor would love nothing more than to be "over it" too.

Unfortunately, the neurobiology of trauma doesn't work that way. Flashbacks, nightmares, and chronic anxiety can take a serious toll on a person. For this reason, authentic relationships that honor a free exchange of emotion must be nurtured during the healing process. Otherwise, the survivor is relegated to putting on a destructive mask every day, pretending everything is fine.

There is nothing more precious to a survivor than a friend or family member's time and patience. I am so grateful for the people our family has met, both before and after the assault, who have stuck by the healed and still-healing versions of us. You stayed when it would have been easier to drift away. You have helped us restore our joy. Because forging human connection and rebuilding trust are at the center of a survivor's journey after rape, I should mention some responses that are helpful when a person discloses their pain following an assault.

I really want to stress that believing the person's story is absolutely paramount. There is no other crime so heavily scrutinized and questioned as rape. Separate yourself from your preconceptions about what rape should "look like" and how someone should act, and instead listen with an open heart.

Acknowledging that the violation occurred and abstaining from blaming the survivor are vital steps in the process. Next, let the person talk about what happened to them, even if it makes you uncomfortable. It is undoubtedly even more agonizing for them. Sit with the survivor, hold space for them, and don't attempt to fix things for them right away. Survivors who disclose assault are not looking for quick, generic solutions and superficial platitudes.

Saying things like "You will be fine" or "It could have been worse" can feel dismissive and minimize their pain when what survivors really need is validation. Assure them of your support and your willingness to help them access the resources they need when they are ready, not on someone else's timeline.

Another substantial loss, or rather, in hindsight, a revelation, in my life was my religious innocence. Trauma reshaped my faith, not by breaking it, but by expanding it. I always naïvely assumed that the brick and mortar walls of a church would be sufficient in keeping evil out and that I would be safe in that setting. That is what the church had always been for me, a physically unshakable shelter. My place of only peace.

As a result of the crimes, however, I learned the hard way that there are no magic boundaries or mandatory loyalties that come attached to the sign on a house of worship. God's love walks around freely inside all of us, and fellowship happens wherever you are able to connect your authentic self with that of another person.

While I continue to receive great comfort from the relationships rooted in my Christian faith, I have also experienced deep, transforming love from strangers, survivors, and helpers outside of it. I have felt the connection inside marginalized communities here in the United States and on random city streets all over the world.

Contrary to what my attacker may have intended, my faith in God's universal and unconditional love for all of humanity is stronger and more vibrant than ever. My trauma expanded my capacity for empathy, and I believe that was one of the greatest gifts to emerge from this journey. My rapist broke my heart, and now it is wide open in the best way. I can love people even deeper.

In all of this, there is one truth I keep coming back to: trauma changes you. Trauma, regardless of its cause, upends everything you may have taken for granted in life. It rocks your foundation and fundamentally transforms you. That is inevitable. The choice that everyone has to make after trauma, however, is how to move forward by integrating this reality into their new sense of self.

In my experience, just papering over it like it never happened was not a sustainable path. In taking that approach, you end up suppressing the powerful lessons that have come out of your experience and eventually become stuck. Growth after trauma is not about erasing the past, but rather reframing it so it can empower your future.

The positive psychological changes I experienced by working through my fears and disappointments have motivated me to find a new purpose in life. I have a deeper and more comprehensive perspective on love and happiness than ever before. With that new viewpoint comes a revised set of life goals that are underpinned by a deep commitment to help others struggling with the scars of sexual violence and to inspire those who work with them.

It has been said that the hallmark of true recovery doesn't simply mean that you can handle the pain of your trauma. Success is also found in your capacity to experience joy again.

Healing is never done in isolation, and loneliness is the enemy. Strong survivors and healthy communities are born out of support networks that acknowledge the presence and effects of crime while working to rebuild those who have been hurt.

Seek out support groups and assistance programs in your neighborhood. If there are none, find online resources where you can connect with people in similar situations. Build bonds in spaces that encourage an atmosphere of trust and authenticity.

Please be patient and gentle with yourself and know that true recovery takes time. Healing is seldom linear. It is a meandering journey with hills and valleys, triumphs and setbacks. You will get there when the time is right and might find great value in sharing part of your walk with others on a similar course. Share your insights, hopes, and dreams with them so that you can lift each other up with dignity and experience deeper joy.

The same realization that reshaped my healing also shaped my mission. When I set out to create an organization where survivors and their families could turn for information and encouragement, I knew I needed to select just the right name. My own personal journey replayed in my head as I brainstormed ideas.

All of a sudden, the answer became crystal clear. I realized that the phrase I seemed to repeat again and again in my presentations would make just the right name for my organization: Not Just Me.

It was not just me that day in the van when I was abducted and raped. My children were victimized as well.

It was not just me who had suffered at the hands of this rapist in the past. It eventually came to light that there were at least four other victims who were violated by this man.

It was not just me who was left reeling from the aftereffects of the sexual assault. I watched my husband, my parents, and other family members and close friends grieve for what they had experienced too.

It was not just me alone who discovered the strength to take my case to trial. During my four-year legal battle, I was supported by numerous advocates, law enforcement personnel, and members of the State Attorney's Office. They kept encouraging me to push toward justice, even when giving up felt like the best thing to do.

And finally, it is not just me who is a victim of rape. The National Crime Victimization Study, completed by the Department of Justice's Bureau of Justice Statistics, reports that a sexual assault is attempted or completed every minute in this country. It also states that 1 in 6 women and 1 in 33 men will be the victims of completed or attempted rape in their lifetime.

I am certainly not alone!

I hold these words, that I first read while looking for services for myself on the Florida Council Against Sexual Assault's (FCASV) website two decades ago, close to my heart: "Anyone can be a victim of sexual violence. Anyone can heal from sexual violence. Everyone can help create a world free of sexual violence."

The story never belonged to me alone, and neither did the healing. In April of 2025, I was both extremely surprised and honored to receive the annual Carrie Morgan Whitcomb Award at the American Society of Crime Lab Directors Conference in Denver, Colorado. I was presented with the President's Coin, which is given in the spirit of the legendary Carrie Whitcomb, the first female director of a federal crime lab in the United States.

The award honors an individual whose work has provided visionary leadership and meaningful support to the forensic science community. In a room filled with scientists, I was humbled to have my lay advocacy as a survivor recognized in such a profound way. It was especially gratifying to receive this award with my son seated in the audience. My children have been my primary motivation for surviving and for thriving since the first moment of this journey.

And so, where do I go from here? I keep showing up. I keep listening. I keep lending my voice wherever it is needed. I keep believing that systems can change when people care enough to act, and that healing multiplies when it is shared.

My story began in violence, but it has never been about violence alone. It has always been about resilience, accountability, and the quiet power of refusing to let harm have the final word.

This work is not finished. But neither am I.

35

Not Just Me

FOR A LONG TIME, I thought this story was about survival. Then I thought it was about justice. It took years for me to understand that it was always about something much bigger than either of those things.

Well before the violence, before the courtroom and the legislation and the years of advocacy that followed, God was already preparing me for a calling I never would have chosen for myself. Looking back now, I can see how nothing in my life was wasted. The education, the relationships, the opportunities, and even the pain were being woven together in ways I could not yet see. The people who showed up at exactly the right moments were not coincidences. They were provision. What happened to me was devastating, but what God has done with it has been redemptive.

For years, I carried the weight of believing this was my story alone. Over time, I realized how untrue that was. Violence never isolates itself to one person. It ripples outward, touching children, spouses, parents, friends, and entire communities. Healing does the same. When one survivor is believed, supported, and restored, the impact reaches far beyond that single life.

It was not just me who survived that night. My children survived it too.

They lost a version of their mother, a sense of safety, a home, and a life that would never return in the same way. And yet, they also gained something that continues to humble me: resilience, compassion, and a front-row seat to what faith looks like when it is lived rather than just spoken.

I am incredibly proud of the people they are becoming and deeply grateful for the grace with which they continue to heal and discover what God has for their lives. My family carried this journey with me in ways both seen and unseen, and I would not be here without them.

This work has taken me into spaces I never imagined I would enter: laboratories and hospitals, courtrooms and classrooms, police departments and legislative chambers. Along the way, I have met extraordinary people, survivors, advocates, scientists, officers, nurses, and lawmakers, each doing their part to push back darkness with truth. None of it happened in isolation. None of it was mean to.

That realization is what gave *Not Just Me* its name.

This story does not belong to me alone. It belongs to every survivor who has wondered if their pain mattered, to every professional who chose compassion over convenience, and to every family learning how to love one another through trauma. It belongs to anyone willing to believe that even the deepest suffering can be transformed into purpose.

If there is one thing I hope you carry with you from these pages, it is this: you are not alone. You never were. Healing is not quick or easy, but it is possible. God is still in the business of restoring what has been broken, and I am living proof of that.

So wherever this story meets you, in pain or in hope, in grief or in healing, I pray that you will choose to believe, to listen, and to stand with those who have been hurt, what we do with suffering matters.

This was never just my story.

And it is not just yours either.

Acknowledgments

WHEN I MAKE A presentation to a forensic lab or show up to speak in a classroom or on Capitol Hill, people always ask me questions about how I got through the horrors of rape and the resulting trial. As a survivor, I am acutely aware that sexual violence is a horribly intimate crime that leaves many to suffer in confusion and isolation. I am extremely grateful to say that my support system made sure that I always felt believed and that I was never left alone in my healing. This book is as much theirs as it is mine.

First and foremost, I would like to say a big thank you to my incredible family who held me in my brokenness and listened to me cry. Your patience with my spirit enabled me to rebuild my life and find joy again. Your love is why I am able to laugh and smile today.

To my husband Jamie, you breathed new life into my heart and body. You helped me see beauty where I once saw only shame and ugliness. You are my safe harbor. Thank you also to my parents, Joe and Susan Diehl. The comfort and care that you provided to all of us in the immediate aftermath of the crime were lifesaving in every way. Helping with the kids, tending to my mental health and medical issues, and offering to be the voice of the family when we were too scared or exhausted to take the reins, meant everything to us.

To my children, Mia and Peter, you lived the most frightening chapters of this narrative right alongside me. This is your story too. You may not have been old enough to fully comprehend the perversion of the acts, but I know you sensed the evil. I love you more than anything and will always lay down my life to protect yours. Your presence with me in the van gave me my reason to fight for survival and my inspiration to fight back in court when it was all over. I am proud of the lives you have created and the adults you have become. You are my heroes.

I would also like to acknowledge my incredible father-in-law and mother-in-law, Carlos and Sally Weil, who immediately boarded a flight from Philadelphia to Miami to help in any way they could during those first few weeks and then again when the case went to trial.

Thanks to my brother Jim Diehl and my sister-in-law Amy Diehl for all of their prayers, emotional support, and offers to help from Texas.

A heartfelt thank you to my brother-in-law and sister-in-law Mike and Thursa Weil who flew in the next day from London, England to help mind the children and take care of our physical needs.

I would like to thank my brother-in-law and sister-in-law Cub and Harris Weil for the steadfast love and care they sent from California. To my nieces and nephews Jacob, Megan, Ian, Betsy, and Olivia. I appreciate how you have all made me smile over the years and provided a much-needed distraction from the trauma. I wish you all a lifetime of love, joy, and safety.

And to my aunts, uncles and cousins who are scattered out across the country, thank you for checking in on us as the weeks and years dragged on. Your love and concern was just what we needed to keep going some days.

I was also blessed to have four active, loving grandparents that gave me a strong foundation in life. Grandpa Doc and Grandma LoLo, and Grandma Alice and Grandpa Joe, I honor you in writing this book. While three of them passed away before I became a mother, my Grandpa Joe lived on for over two decades after my assault. He passed away shortly before his 102nd birthday, always claiming to be my biggest fan and encouraging me to write a book someday. I hope he is smiling down from heaven now that it is complete.

I would also like to acknowledge the people of Miami for springing into action after the crime. The community response was very encouraging and the sexual assault protocols that were already in place made the difficult moments I encountered more tolerable. Everyone from the first responders, sex crimes detectives, specialized forensic nurses and doctors at the Roxcy Bolton Rape Treatment Center and skilled advocates worked like a well-oiled machine to provide competent, compassionate care. During the crucial days after my assault, I felt well cared for and confident that whatever evidence was left behind by my rapist would be expertly preserved for trial.

Thank you to the Village of Palmetto Bay, Pinecrest, and the surrounding areas for keeping the wanted posters up for almost six months and to the MDPD for putting together a taskforce to add more muscle to the case. This case never grew cold or stagnant thanks to you and the FDLE.

And to my State Attorney, Laura Adams, you are a true warrior in all of this. You believed in the case, never took your foot off the pedal, and encouraged me to go to trial alone when I declined the plea deal. There is no closure for me in all of this without you.

I mention in the book how special my little corner of metropolitan Miami is to me and how it provided me with everything I ever needed growing up in terms of education, opportunities, and friends. I will always be especially grateful to my junior high school creative writing teacher, Veda Levin, and legendary high school debate coach, Fran Berger. They both left an indelible mark on my life before the crime and provided me with the necessary writing and speaking skills to use during my recovery and in my advocacy.

My friends are the jewels that crown this story because they are the glue that stuck around to hold me as I evolved back into myself. To my friends from childhood, thank you for rallying around me in our adult years and helping me get my foundation established. Your support of my mission has been invaluable.

At the time of our abduction, I was part of a special playgroup at my church with outstanding moms who truly cared about each other and about each other's children. A few of them went above and beyond the call of duty and, for months, ran meal trains, took my kids out for playdates, brought me care packages, and sat with me while I was alone and scared. I call this group of "sisters" my Same Sweet Girls. Tina, Loralynn, Laura, and Stephanie, you are angels here on earth and I am so happy that after 20+ years, you are still cheering me on.

In Palm Beach County, especially in Jupiter, there are many important people to acknowledge as well. I moved here within months of the assault and relied on trusted members of my new community to help me heal and get through the four long years awaiting trial. Many of these people have sustained me throughout my years of advocacy and activism, as well.

First, thank you to my compassionate therapist, Dr. Laura Robinson, who has guided me for decades. I would also like to thank my tribe of mom friends from Jerry Thomas Elementary school and my dear friends from the PTO Board, Vicky, Nancy, and Lori (aka The Boss, RIP) who supported me emotionally but also helped me find fun and purpose outside of my trauma.

To Howard and Jupiter Traditional Martial Arts, thank you for doing over a decade of self-defense classes at the community center and allowing me to come talk about the importance of situational awareness.

To Palm Beach County Victim Services, I am beyond blessed to partner with you in bringing impactful events to individuals in the county and providing much-needed supplies for survivors seen at Butterfly House. Our county is so lucky to have you and your phenomenal programs that help with healing and justice.

The advocacy I have been able to do gives real purpose to my life now. It shows that progress can be a valuable byproduct of extreme pain. I want to thank the companies, schools and organizations that see value in sharing the survivor experience. From large corporations that advance DNA and other identification technology to criminal justice and forensic science programs at colleges and universities nationwide, I am always grateful for your invitations to speak, and hopefully inspire, your employees and students.

This deep appreciation extends to SANE nursing programs, DNA labs, law enforcement training centers, and government entities like the FBI and Congress, that continue to acknowledge the wisdom in a victim's voice. By collaborating and lifting one another up, we can improve the lives of sexual assault survivors and hopefully work to prevent this hideous crime.

If any reader desires to learn more about these issues, please reach out to me at www.notjustmefoundation.org. I am committed to being here for you.

Resources

IF YOU OR SOMEONE you know needs help, support is available through the resources listed below. If you are in immediate danger, call 911.

National Sexual Assault Hotline – 800.656.HOPE (4673)
The hotline provides emotional support, advice and crisis intervention and through local partnerships callers can receive immediate help in their community.

National Sexual Assault Online Hotline – online.rainn.org
The online hotline provides support, advice, and crisis intervention through a secure instant-messaging format. For help in Spanish, visit rainn.org/es.

Americans Overseas Domestic Violence Crisis Center and the Sexual Assault Support & Help for Americans Abroad Program – 866.USWOMEN (879.6636)
The crisis center can be reached internationally toll-free from 175 countries, serving both civilian and military populations overseas. Advocates can be reached 24/7 by first dialing your AT&T USADirect access number and at the prompt, enter the phone number: 866-USWOMEN (879-6636).

Additional Resources

Rape, Abuse, and Incest National Network

RAINN is the nation's largest antisexual assault organization and a national leader in online crisis intervention services. RAINN operates the National Sexual Assault Hotline and the National Sexual Assault Online Hotline. All services are free, confidential, and available.

24/7. https://rainn.org

National Sexual Violence Resource Center

NSVRC supports organizations that provide direct services to sexual assault victims, including; rape crisis centers; national, state, and local agencies; and allied programs.

https://nsvrc.org/find-help/

Joyful Heart Foundation

The mission of the Joyful Heart Foundation is to transform society's response to sexual assault, domestic violence, and child abuse, support survivors' healing, and end this violence forever. Their website details rape kit tracking in all states.

https://joyfulheartfoundation

About the Author

JULIE WEIL IS A sexual assault survivor and global advocate who has transformed personal tragedy into meaningful, lasting change. After enduring a four-year journey through the criminal justice system, her perseverance, alongside the dedicated work of a Miami-based sexual assault nurse examiner, law enforcement agents, a DNA lab team, and the State Attorney's Office, led to her perpetrator receiving seven life sentences.

Rather than stepping away after sentencing, Julie stepped forward.

In 2010, she founded the Not Just Me Foundation to educate communities and improve how sexual assault survivors are treated within the justice system. Her advocacy has led to tangible reform at local, state, federal, and international levels.

Locally, Julie inspired the creation of Butterfly House, Palm Beach County's forensic exam center, and continues to sponsor community awareness initiatives through her foundation. In Florida, she played a key role in the passage of three pieces of legislation addressing the rape kit backlog, including a statewide audit, mandatory testing of all kits, and the implementation of a tracking system.

At the federal level, Julie spent more than two years educating members of Congress about the national rape kit backlog. Her efforts contributed to the passage of the SAFER Act in 2013, now part of the Violence Against Women Act (VAWA). She continues to speak out on Capitol Hill about the need to improve support services for survivors nationally.

Her advocacy extends beyond the United States. Julie worked to help establish Egypt's first rape crisis center and attended its opening in 2016. She has also assisted in training law enforcement agencies and forensic nurses and has spoken internationally, including in Mexico and Canada, on the importance of DNA in solving violent crimes.

Julie's expanding mission now includes advancing awareness around emerging forensic science tools, including biometric identification systems, and encouraging the responsible collection and use of all forms of forensic evidence to support justice and public safety.

Julie's deepest passion is equipping forensic nurses, law enforcement professionals, lab analysts, and victim advocates with the encouragement and resolve to continue fighting for justice. Her life stands as testimony that survivors can become powerful agents of change.

Julie has been featured on CNN, C-SPAN, HLN, and major national news networks. She appeared in the Discovery Channel's *Surviving Evil* and the Biography Channel's *I Survived....* The television news feature "Julie's Fight for Change" earned two Suncoast Emmy Awards. Her story has also been highlighted in *People*, *Ms.*, and *Oxygen* magazines, as well as on podcasts with the National Crime Prevention Council.

Julie's advocacy has also been recognized with numerous honors over the years. These include the Heart of a Woman Award from Aid to Victims of Domestic Abuse presented to her by #MeToo founder Tarana Burke, the Survivor Activist Award from the Florida Council Against Sexual Violence, the Stamp of Courage Award from the Florida Attorney General's Office, the Special Courage Award from the Miami Gardens Police Department, and a Special Award from the National Organization for Women (Palm Beach County chapter) for her work fighting violence against women and inspiring the creation of Butterfly House.

Her advocacy was also nationally recognized through USA Network's Characters Unite Award, nominated by RAINN for her work addressing the rape kit backlog. Earlier in her advocacy career, she also received the Outstanding Programming for Chapter Presentations Award from Moms' Clubs International for her "Keeping Moms Safe" program. In addition, the Palm Beach County Sexual Assault Response Team (SART) that she helped inspire received the Florida Council Against Sexual Violence Sexual Assault Response Team of the Year Award for its work improving community responses for survivors. Most recently, Julie was honored with the 2025 Carrie Whitcomb Award for her continued leadership and advocacy on behalf of survivors.

Through advocacy, education, and unwavering courage, Julie continues to ensure that no survivor feels alone and that justice systems work better for those they are meant to protect.

www.ingramcontent.com/pod-product-compliance
Lightning Source LLC
LaVergne TN
LVHW091122080826
845145LV00008B/2013